WHEN
WIVES WALK
IN
Grace

WHEN WIVES WALK IN
Grace

STEVE McVEY

HARVEST HOUSE PUBLISHERS
EUGENE, OREGON

Cover by Left Coast Design, Portland, Oregon

Cover photo © Yuri Arcurs / Shutterstock

This book contains stories in which people's names and some details of their situations have been changed to protect their privacy.

WHEN WIVES WALK IN GRACE
Copyright © 2013 by Steve McVey
Published by Harvest House Publishers
Eugene, Oregon 97402
www.harvesthousepublishers.com

McVey, Steve
    When wives walk in grace / Steve McVey.
        pages cm
    ISBN 978-0-7369-5235-4 (pbk.)
    ISBN 978-0-7369-5236-1 (eBook)
    1. Wives—Religious life. 2. Mothers—Religious life. 3. Christian women—Religious life. I. Title.
    BV4528.15.M47 2013
    248.8'435—dc23

                                                                    2012048515

Printed in the United States of America

13 14 15 16 17 18 19 20 21 / VP-JH / 10 9 8 7 6 5 4 3 2 1

To Agape, *whose sunrise tranquility, gentle pitch, and soft, sweet melody of breath through her rigging awakened this book in me.*

To Jan, Carol, and Melanie, whose feminine affirmation of early chapters convinced me that the Breath giving voice to this book was real.

And to Roger and Al, whose amen backed the verdict of their wives.

Acknowledgments

As with each book I've written, *When Wives Walk in Grace* is a team effort. The initial motivation for the book has been all the wives who have asked me questions about marriage as I've traveled in ministry for almost 20 years. Your transparency and hunger to know your Father's heart on these issues were the seminal inspiration for what you now hold in your hand.

Appreciation for the hardworking team at Harvest House Publishers is an ever-present reality for me. So many people there have a hand in the making of a book, and I'm indebted to them all. I especially appreciate Gene Skinner, my editor for this book. His encouragement and editing skills have made it a better book.

I want to thank my Grace Walk team, those who stand with such enthusiasm to share the message of grace around the world. They aren't just co-laborers in the ministry, but are each dear friends who fan the flame in me constantly. What a thrill to serve together with such a great group! I can't imagine this journey without them.

Deep gratitude to my most precious treasure, Melanie. Her encouragement and suggestions have been of inestimable value with this book. As this book is released, we'll be celebrating 40 years of marriage. Wow, what lottery in heaven did I win!

Finally, my greatest thanks to the One who has put it all into place. None of it would matter without Him. He is the true Author and Finisher of my life, and to Him I give the greatest glory and praise. Thank You, Father.

Contents

Foreword 9

Introduction 11

1 Kissing Frogs 13

2 Solo Spirituality 21

3 Second Thoughts 29

4 Intrinsic Value 37

5 Bible Bangers 45

6 Soured Saints 53

7 Unholy Ghosts 61

8 Confronting Bullies 69

9 Trash Talk 77

10 Greener Grass 85

11 Rearing Children 93

12 Festering Wounds 101

13 Religious Arguments 109

14 Other Voices 117

15 Clean Fights 125

16 Juggling Acts 135

17 Prodigal Sons 143

18 Blended Families 151

19 Unscrambling Eggs 159

20 Physical Abuse 167

21 Emotional Absence 177

22 Unfailing Love 189

A Personal Word 195

Discussion Questions 197

Foreword

Finally, a book written for women! I've always told Steve this was his specialty. After years of Steve counseling women, of studying, of teaching and preaching, this book has finally come about.

Steve and I have counseled women and prayed with them about their marriages, their children, their parents, and their in-laws; about abuse and betrayal, about hurts, failures, and disappointments. It's more than could be discussed in this one book, but one thing was always clear to me. I could listen with sympathy and compassion, I could hold hands and give hugs, I could cry with them...but the one thing I did not have was the gifting to see into the very heart of their problems. I could not see the truth that lay beneath all the shouting, the finger-pointing, the tears, and the lies. Not so with Steve. He has always had the ability to cut through to the heart of the matter. He is able to move all the clutter to the side and uncover the heart of the issue.

When Wives Walk in Grace is for women who need help—real help. Not trite words spoken in a religious, almost robotic way. Not someone quoting Scripture to them about the kind of Proverbs 31 wives they should be regardless of the kind of man they are living with.

You will find that this book cuts through all the empty Bible babble that's out there and points you toward a loving God who embraces you and will carry you through the terrible times when you don't have a clue what to do or where to turn.

I know the thoughts many women have. "Men have always abused me in one way or another. I can't trust a man to give me the answers I need. I just can't listen to a man right now."

I understand that kind of thinking, having been abused by men myself at a very young age. It took me many years to find the healing that our Father offers and that my husband loved into me. I believe that this book has been written in such a way that you will hear the voice of your loving heavenly Father. You will know in your very soul that God Himself has spoken to you through the words written here.

Trust our loving God—that He led you to this book and that in it you will find many of the answers you have been seeking. Steve is a man of wisdom and integrity. He loves the Lord with his whole heart and loves people (me most of all!). It is from that baseline that he writes. You will see that he is a man you can trust—one who will not give you pat answers to your most difficult problems. I believe that as you read, you will hear real answers for very real circumstances.

I pray that *When Wives Walk in Grace* finds its way into the hands of women everywhere who struggle to be loved, to be heard, and to be valued. This is the book for which many have long waited. No book can give every answer to every problem, but this one will certainly take you to the One who does have all the answers.

May our loving and gracious heavenly Father bless you and complete the work He has begun in you. This book will help you discover the life God intends you to have—one of peace and joy.

Melanie McVey
Atlanta, Georgia

Introduction

I became a senior pastor in 1973 and have counseled wives for thousands of hours in the ensuing years. Since I left the local pastorate in 1994 and began traveling as an itinerate speaker, I have had the opportunity to speak to wives on six continents. I have noticed that across the world, these wives have asked me almost identical questions about their marriages. This fact has convinced me that the problems wives face today are universal.

As I helped women understand how the sufficiency of Christ is the key to seeing transformation in their marriages, I began to see that this book could fill a need. I realize that a multitude of books address marriage, and I affirm that many of those books have much good to offer. However, this book isn't like some of the self-improvement books that challenge the reader to personal change.

Unlike other books on the subject, *When Wives Walk in Grace* doesn't present behavioral prescriptions for strengthening your marriage. You certainly will find much practical direction in these pages, but the underlying theme of this book is that Jesus Christ can transform and strengthen your marriage by His grace. Principles don't produce miracles. But there is one Person who can transform anybody's life or home.

As you read this book, ask the Spirit of Christ within you to speak to you. As you trust Him, you will find yourself growing in hope, in practical knowledge, and in faith that your marriage can be the relationship your Father intends for you to enjoy. The One who gave Adam and Eve to each other as gifts wants you and your husband to know and enjoy the gift He has given to each of you. Many wives have seen their marriages transformed by the things you will learn here. I pray that God's Spirit will lead you into that same sort of divine transformation.

1

Kissing Frogs

’ve been on a zillion diets. A lot of men wouldn’t admit that, but I’ll acknowledge it to make a point here. It’s not something I’ve been pleased about or successful doing for long. Even as I write these words, I would like to zap away the weight. It’s just the way it has been for me all my adult life. Through the years I looked for the perfect diet, one I could live with indefinitely so I could keep the weight off. Every time I started a new one, I thought, “If I can just follow this regimen, I should be able to keep off the weight.” The problem was that my if-then scenario never worked out the way I hoped it would.

You’re probably familiar with the Atkins diet—the low-carbohydrate, high-protein approach. One day while I was on that particular diet and had deprived myself of carbohydrates for weeks, I discovered something so wonderful it almost brought tears to my eyes—Russell Stover sugar-free, low-carb chocolates. I had avoided chocolate for so long that I secretly feared I might never know such carnal pleasure again.

Then Russell Stover came to me. In the depths of my dieter’s despair, he lifted me up from my sweetless wasteland and set my feet on chocolate ground. May his name be blessed! Russell Stover delivered me from the prison of chocolate deprivation.

Long had there been civil unrest in the depths of my soul as my dictatorial and determined dieter's will held me in slavery. My unbridled yearning for chocolate had regularly chanted, "We shall overcome." Now at last my appetite cried out, "Free at last! Free at last! Thank God Almighty, I'm free at last!"

When I discovered these chocolates, I thought the millennial reign surely had begun. I felt as if the wrongs of the earth had righted themselves and all of life made sense again. The famine was over, and chocolate had returned to its rightful place in my life.

I bought low-carb caramels, a low-carb version of Butterfingers, low-carb peanut butter cups, low-carb chocolate-covered peanuts, and even a low-carb version of M&M's. It was a dieter's nirvana. With those first bites of chocolate, I savored the delicacy. Then for the next week, I ate it with no restraint—freely enjoying it with an innocence I believed hadn't been known since Adam and Eve walked naked in the garden and were not ashamed. After all, it was *low carb*!

I gorged on this cocoa-manna from heaven. I felt that truly I was experiencing life the way it was meant to be enjoyed. I never varied from my previous low-carb routine at mealtime. But between meals, Russell Stover low-carb chocolates and I became best friends.

When Monday rolled around and it was time for my self-imposed weekly weigh-in, I stepped out of the shower and onto the scales with no fear at all. After all, I was on a low-carb diet that surely had been working for me. But as I looked down at the number on the scales, I was shocked. I assumed I was misreading the digital display. I stepped off the scales to give them a moment to reset, and then I stepped back on again. The number was the same. My heart sank. Anxiety suddenly flooded my emotions, and the fat demons of the universe taunted me: "Gotcha, sucker! You gained more weight this week than you lost in the previous two weeks!"

"What happened?" Those words bounced around inside my fat head in derision. "I ate low carbs this week!" I protested. "*If* I eat low carbs, *then* I'm supposed to lose weight every week! That's how this thing works!" I thought. Then it hit me. "The candy! Could it be the low-carb candy?" I quickly dressed and went immediately to the kitchen to read the nutrition panel on the bags again to make sure my memory of the carb count was correct.

As I stood there in the kitchen, barely dressed and with my wet hair still sticking straight up, I anxiously studied the nutrition information on the back of the candy bags. Then I saw it—the other column, the one that listed serving size and calories per serving. I was shocked.

Suddenly the scales made sense. I had indeed eaten low-carb meals all week. But with this candy, I had eaten enough calories to feed a family of three for a week in some poverty-stricken countries. It was a lesson hard learned—low net carbohydrates might still mean a lot of calories.

I thought that if I ate a low-carbohydrate diet, I would still lose weight. Was I ever wrong! "*If* I do this, *then* that will happen." Most of us take that approach in many areas of our lives, and then we feel complete frustration or even anger when things don't work out the way we had hoped.

Of Frogs and Princes

Do you know the story about the young maiden who kissed a frog that turned into a prince? Well, it's a fairy tale. The real world is quite different. Take it from a guy who for 40 years has counseled a multitude of women about their relationships with men. Sometimes the real-life story is just the opposite from the fairy tale. More times than you might think, women feel as if they kissed a prince, but after they married him, he gradually turned into a toad. They came into marriage with high expectations, but as time passed, things didn't turn out at all the way they had hoped.

Maybe you bought this book out of a sense of despair about your marriage. You may desperately want to see your husband change but wonder if it's even possible. If so, I have bad news and good news. The bad news is that a wife can't turn a toad into a prince regardless of how hard she tries, how much she prays, or how badly she wants to. No wife has that kind of power.

The good news is that even though *you* can't change your husband, he *can* be changed. By stepping away from the fairy-tale metaphor and into biblical truth, we can see the situation in a much more hopeful light. Your husband can be transformed. It may take a miracle, but thankfully, God is a miracle worker who can do what needs to be done in you, in your husband, and in your marriage. The One who created your man knows better than anyone else (including you) how he thinks and functions.

Not a Prescription, but a Person

In this book, I'm going to tell you some things that I've seen put to the test and that have worked. The reason for that is simple. I'm not going to give you a prescription for a strong marriage. Instead, I'm going to guide you to the Person who has a long track record of healing and restoring sick and broken people and relationships. Nobody is beyond the reach of God's amazing grace. Even if we run from God, eventually we discover that we can't outrun Him. I tell you this to give you assurance and hope. God can capture your husband's attention and do what He wants to do with him.

If you feel a sense of desperation about the way your husband behaves or doesn't behave, take heart. God cares about him even more than you do, and He cares about your marriage too. Maybe your husband is a believer, or maybe he isn't. We'll discuss both scenarios. God is big. In fact, He is bigger than the most stubborn person alive. So if you're wondering whether your husband can ever truly change, embrace hope now. He can't change himself, but he can be changed by the One who created him. Let your desperation give way to a renewed hope in God.

Maybe you aren't feeling the kind of desperation I've just described. Perhaps you just want a stronger shared faith between you and your husband, but you're frustrated. Like me on the Atkins diet, you thought you were doing all the right things. You've read other books about marriage. You've read your Bible and prayed about your relationship with your husband. You've put in the work. You've tried to talk to your husband. Maybe you've even cried about your marriage at times. You've done all you know to do, and things still haven't changed. Now, you may not be desperate, but you are discouraged.

Let me assure you that you're not alone. My motivation for writing this book comes from this one need. I travel in ministry much of the time, and almost everywhere I go, wives want to talk to me about their marriages and children. Many are sincere Christian ladies who are frustrated because their husbands don't share their spiritual passion. They grieve the fact that their husbands aren't as "spiritual" as they want them to be. They imagine what life would be like if their husbands were the kind of godly men they want them to become.

Others are in dire situations and don't know what to do. They face physically abusive husbands, husbands who are emotionally absent, and husbands who try to get them to do things that are blatantly sinful. I'll address these and other such scenarios in this book.

If-Then Thinking

Some situations are more serious than others, but there is a common error many wives make. They believe that *if* they can only discover what to do to help their husbands become the men they ought to be, *then* life will correct itself and things will be fine. To their dismay, the if-then expectation they've imposed on their marriages isn't working out so far. Most haven't given up though. They think they simply need to find the right approach and come at the situation again from a different angle and with renewed vigor.

I always feel sorry for these wives. If grades were given for sincere effort, they certainly would make the dean's list. The problem is that regardless of what they do or how well they do it, they can't change their husbands. It's just not going to happen. Only God can do that, and He'll do it in His time and in His way. Waiting for your mate to change can be maddening when you feel as if it's never going to happen.

If you've felt that way about your husband, this book will encourage you. I'm not going to offer you tips on how to change your husband. That's not what you need. Rather, I'll offer you hope based on the nature of your loving Father and on biblical truth. This book is filled with practical biblical guidelines, but it won't give you a silver bullet to end everything you think is wrong in your home and instantly make it right. Let's be honest. That's not realistic. Instead, I'll give you a platform of grace to stand on and a practical approach in relating to your husband while you wait for your Father to bring the transformation to your marriage you want to see. I'll also help you know what to do and what not to do in the meantime.

Although the title of this book suggests it is directed to wives, there will also be discussion here about rearing children. Much tension is created in marriages because of the stress associated with children. Several chapters will speak from different angles to the matter of parenting.

Grace Versus Self-Help

Grace—that's the key. Grace can be described in many ways, but for our purpose here, we will define it as the miraculous ability you possess (because of Christ living inside you) to be, do, and say the most helpful and effective things possible to move toward a strong marriage and family.

It's not about you and your knowledge or ability to change the situation by doing the right thing. That's not grace at all. That's called self-help and is an expression of a fleshly and counterproductive self-sufficiency. There's a lot of that kind of talk going around in the modern church world, but it's not going to work. I hope that you've had enough of the methods prescribed by the religious gurus of our day and that you know firsthand that they don't work. If so, you're already ahead in the game because you realize that formulas for changing your marriage are misguided and doomed to fail every time.

I hope you don't think you just need to try harder or pray more or do something different. Again, it's not about you and your efforts. When things change (and they will), it will be obvious to you that God was the One who did it. That's the way grace works.

Jesus in You

The key here is Jesus Christ. It's all about what He wants to do—first in you, then in your marriage relationship, and finally in your parenting approach. Notice the order. It has to start with you personally. You won't be passive through this process. Christ will empower your actions as He works through you and in your home. I'm not suggesting that your husband doesn't need to change. I'm simply saying that you can't change him. Not now or ever.

If, on the other hand, you find your own attitudes and actions about your marriage being changed, you might be surprised by what ends up happening in your relationship. Frustration, conflict, or disillusionment in a marriage make it hard to see things clearly.

As you read through this book, your disillusionment will be displaced by hope. You will be equipped with grace-based truths and specific, helpful steps of faith. These grace-based truths and steps aren't principles per se. That's too academic and sterile. Marriages aren't built on formulas regardless of how good they are. Rather, we will discuss actual expressions of Christ working out His life in your marriage relationship. "Unless the LORD builds the house, the work of the builders is wasted" (Psalm 127:1 NLT). How true. Christ is the One who has to do it, or you're sunk. The good news is that He *does* intend to do it.

So we're going to discuss how to let Him build up your marriage and strengthen you as a parent. I assure you that the things suggested in this book won't simply be theoretical ideas. I will present you with very practical ideas in each chapter. I will offer you direction about certain things you can do, but you'll do them in the power of Christ's indwelling life and not by sheer self-determination. That difference may not sound like much now, but it's actually *huge*, and you'll see that clearly as we progress.

How do you change a frog into a prince? You don't—but God can. Do you believe that? Okay then, are you ready to move forward? It all begins with the matter of whether God really cares about what's going on in your marriage right now. Sometimes it seems as if He must not, or He would do something to change things. But things are often very different from the way they seem.

2

Solo Spirituality

Barb grew up in a healthy home, and her mom and dad were obviously in love. Her dad was an elder in their local church, and her mom taught the young couples' Bible study. "When the doors were opened, we were there," she says.

Due to the way her own family always functioned, Barb took it for granted that a Christian husband does certain things. First and foremost, he takes his family to church every week. To her, that was a given in a Christian home. She held other expectations about what a Christian man does at home too. Traditional things, such as saying the prayer before meals, leading the family in a daily "family altar" of reading the Bible and praying together, talking about life in terms of spiritual realities…these weren't monumental acts to her. They were the normal and routine things that Christian families experienced under the leadership of godly men.

Barb met Zack during her sophomore year in college. He was playing the guitar and leading choruses at Young Life meetings on campus. She immediately was attracted to Zack. He had a good sense of humor. He seemed comfortable with his faith and related easily to the people around him. Zack was the son of a pastor and seemed to have grown up pretty much the way she had.

Zack asked Barb to go to a Christian concert with him for their first date. Over the next two years, they were inseparable. Before long, they both realized they wanted to spend their lives together, and so they began making wedding preparations. A few months after graduation, on a warm Saturday afternoon in June, Zack's dad performed the ceremony.

Barb's dreams were immersed in and inseparable from her new life with Zack. She saw nothing but bright days ahead. Zack began a career in a sales position with a successful company. He was soon breaking sales records and distinguishing himself in exceptional ways through his sales skills.

Barb was proud of him. The bonuses and salary increases were great. Barb also enjoyed the trips Zack won at work through his achievements.

After 18 months, Barb found out she was going to have a baby, and they were both thrilled. But one thing was bothering Barb, and she thought she and Zach should discuss it since they would soon have a child. Barb's concern was that their spiritual lives seemed to be in a gradual decline.

Because of Zack's demanding work schedule, he often said that he was too tired to go to church on Sunday and that he wanted the two of them to just rest and enjoy the day together. Barb wasn't completely comfortable missing church because she had been taught all her life that attendance was important, but she did enjoy those relaxed Sundays together. But now things were different. In her mind, since they were going to have a baby, changes were needed. "We need to get back in church," she mentioned to Zack one Sunday afternoon.

She couldn't have been more surprised by his response. "Barb, I understand your concern, but I'm in a different place now than I was when we were first married," he explained. "You know my spiritual life is real to me, but God has put me where I am so I can provide for you and for our baby. My work is demanding. I'll do the best I can, but I may need you to step up on the home front for a while when it comes to spiritual things. Sunday is the only day I can actually rest, and that's what I want to do."

For the first time in their marriage, Barb began to be afraid about her husband's spiritual condition. She had always believed that for a husband to be the spiritual leader wasn't optional, and now she was hearing Zack delegate this important responsibility to her.

Their baby girl was born, and less than two years later, they learned that a son was on the way. Barb and Zack continued to be deeply in love, but by the time the children were beginning school, Barb felt that Zack had abandoned all responsibility for spiritual leadership at home. She was the one who said prayers with the children at night. She took them to church alone most of the time. She felt as if the only spiritual influence her children ever saw at home was from her, and that bothered her greatly.

Does God Care?

By the time I met Barb, she and Zach had been married ten years. She was discouraged and wondering aloud with me about what to do. "I don't get it," she said. "I grew up in a godly home with a godly dad. Zack grew up in a godly home. He knows better than this. I've talked and talked and talked to him about it, but it does no good. I've prayed about it, but nothing changes. I've wondered why God won't change Zack. If He *can*, why won't He? Sometimes it seems like I care more about my husband's spiritual condition than God does."

I knew Barb didn't really believe that, but I also knew she honestly felt that way at times. She wanted to see God's Spirit move in Zack's life and change him. She had prayed for that for a number of years, but nothing ever happened. Given her background, it seemed reasonable for her to wonder if God really cared. Was she destined to spend her life as the spiritual leader, married to a man who apparently didn't care much about that part of life anymore?

I've shared Barb's story because your story may be much like hers. The details may differ, but the underlying story is common. I hear it all the time. She marries him. She envisions that they will grow together spiritually, but after a while, he seems to lose interest in spiritual things.

Maybe your marriage scenario is similar. In the next chapter, I'll address women whose husbands have never shown any spiritual interest. But for now, I want to speak to those whose husbands seem to have lost interest in their walk with God. What's a wife to do? Talking about it obviously doesn't work. Pleading with him to step up and lead spiritually doesn't work. In fact, sometimes that causes a man to pull back even more. So what is the answer?

The answer may surprise you: Stop trying to change him. Giving him CDs with biblical teaching from your favorite speaker, telling him all about what's going on at church, trying to entice him with your enthusiasm…these things aren't working, and chances are, they're not going to work.

Personal Space

Here's an important principle to understand that could help you avoid delaying the very thing you want to see. When we feel as if somebody is crowding into our personal space, we will automatically and usually unconsciously step back. It's a defense mechanism built into all of us. None of us like to have other people push their way into our space. If we invite them, that's one thing. But when we haven't invited them into an area of our lives and they intrude anyway, we become uncomfortable, and the situation seldom has a positive outcome. If we don't really care about the person, we may push back. But if it's somebody we do care about, we typically just step back and try to reestablish our personal space as gently as possible.

This "you push in and I'll step back" reflex occurs in your marriage too. You may mean well by stepping into the space reserved for your husband and his God, but you don't belong there unless you're invited. I don't mean to suggest that husbands and wives don't share their walk with Christ together. Rather, I'm suggesting that you cannot force intimacy between your husband and Christ like a religious matchmaker just because you see its value. He has to see it too, and only the Holy Spirit can make that happen.

Outward Versus Inward Change

Depending on your personality and your relationship with your husband, you might be able to influence him to a greater level of external religious behavior, but would that really accomplish what you want? If he did the outward things you want him to do but his heart wasn't in them, would there be real value in that? You may think that at least your children would benefit, but in the long run, they would not. Children can easily distinguish what's real from what's artificial when it comes to this sort of thing.

Far too many families go through religious motions without an authentic and vibrant relationship with Jesus Christ. You don't want your husband or your family to be like that. You want Christ to be real in your home, and for that to happen, you're going to have to wait for Him to be One who brings the result you long to see.

So give up thinking that you can make something happen. Your heavenly Father loves your husband even more than you do, and despite all external evidence to the contrary, He hasn't forgotten about him. Your Father is acting in your husband's life at this very moment, working out things in his heart and head that you don't know anything about. Philippians 1:6 says, "For I am confident of this very thing, that He who began a good work in you will perfect it until the day of Christ Jesus." That promise applies not only to you but also to your husband, so you can be confident that God will continue His work in your husband's life.

In fact, he may not even be aware of what God's Spirit is doing in his life right now. That's okay. Unlike us, God never gets hyped up or panicked about a situation. He usually does His thing quietly, consistently, and miraculously until that which He has decreed happens. And it *will* happen; you can be assured of that. Nobody wins a tug-of-war contest with Almighty God—not even your husband, regardless of how stubborn he may seem. God always wins. That's a big benefit in being God.

So be patient and put your eyes on your Father instead of your husband. You may think he needs to do the external things that he stopped doing, but that isn't the core issue. What he's doing and what he isn't doing isn't the heart of the matter. The real question is, what is going on in his heart?

If you try to convince your husband to do the things you think he ought to be doing, you're missing the real issue. When you talk to him about his spiritual walk, don't focus on the externals. Assuming that you two have a history of comfortably sharing your hearts and minds together, talk to him about what you are experiencing in your relationship to God. Then you can ask him to tell you what is going on spiritually with him.

Remember, his religious behavior is not what's most important. His personal interaction and relationship with God are the primary things. Don't make the mistake of focusing on the symptoms while ignoring the heart of the matter. Talk freely and honestly about your respective walks with God, but be sure that you don't project onto your husband what you believe his relationship to God should look like. We are all individuals who have individual walks with Him.

Comfortable Conversations

After you have developed the habit of discussing your spiritual lives (not your religious activity) together, you will be more likely to find a good time to discuss ways to nurture your collective walk as a family. The key is to avoid putting the cart before the horse. Make sure that you two are completely comfortable and open in discussing your relationship to God before you talk about external expressions of your faith together. Otherwise, you're just putting a Band-Aid on a problem that may never be resolved.

I've seen wives push their husbands to go to church. They believe that is the litmus test of spirituality. Others want their husbands to behave more religiously at home. They want them to read the Bible to the children or pray at meals or do something else that the wives believe a Christian husband should do. There is certainly nothing wrong with those things, but is that really all you want? Wouldn't you rather see Christ transform your husband so that he leads your family with a passion for Christ and for his family's spiritual welfare? He won't become interested in spiritual things just because you remind him of all the things he should be doing. So don't.

I know that's easier said than done, but it is essential that you understand the wisdom of this. I have a reason for laying out this prescription for frustrated wives at the beginning of this book. It's the nature of the flesh in all of us to become control freaks over things we care passionately about, and I know you care passionately about your husband's spiritual well-being. So does God, so let Him be who He is to your husband. He will reveal Himself in His own way and in His own time.

You Can't, but God Can

Maybe you've tried to change your husband enough times to see that you can't do it. If so, then stop trying harder to make something happen and simply *trust God* to work it out based on His plan and power. Your Father can do what you can never do. He can get in your husband's head. He can stir up his heart. He can control his external circumstances. He can move heaven and earth to get the result He wants.

You've begun to read this book because you want to see your heavenly Father change your husband, but could He possibly want to change you too? Before the change comes to your husband's life, could He want you to give up any effort to control this situation?

Might He be inviting you to simply surrender your husband into His loving hands?

I've spoken plainly in this chapter about resigning your position as coordinator of your husband's spiritual condition. I assume that you want the truth and that you don't mind me plainly stating the most important thing first. To keep first things first, it's important for you to internalize what you've read in this chapter and appropriate it to your life. You don't have to feel like doing it to do it. You just need to recognize the truth and respond in faith to what the Holy Spirit is showing you. You can't change your husband, so stop trying. It's that simple. Not easy, but simple. Why not pray right now and ask your Father to enable you to entrust your husband to Him? That simple act of faith may have more impact on your situation than you could possibly imagine.

"Then what do I do?" you may wonder. I will address that question in the chapters ahead, but before you can properly apply the answers to your own life, it's important to surrender your husband's spiritual condition into the hands of God. Otherwise, you'll be likely to take actions I suggest and use them like formulas to change your husband. That won't work. Instead, you must first *give up* your husband into the Father's hands so that He can *take up* the situation and do His work. Sometimes a man can't hear God's voice because his wife's voice is drowning Him out. Give your husband to Him. Then watch and wait. He will work in your husband's life in His way and His timing.

Second Thoughts

"How can something become the right thing when it clearly started out as the wrong thing? Traveling the wrong way on a street can never lead to the right destination, no matter what you do," Linda said to me during her counseling appointment. She and Tom had been married for six years when her mom died at a relatively young age. Her mother's death had caused Linda to rethink the things she valued in life. Unlike Tom, she had grown up in a Christian home and had begun to follow Christ at an early age.

Like many youth, when Linda moved away to college, she drifted away from the anchoring truths she had learned at home. She had always been taught that dating an unbeliever—being "unequally yoked"—would be a serious mistake. But by the time she met Tom at a fraternity party, rules from home about whom to date and whom not to date were the last things on her mind. Tom was fun to be with. He seemed to value her and make her feel good about herself. He often told her how beautiful she was. He made her laugh. Little by little, she found herself falling in love with him.

As their relationship became more and more serious, she had wondered at times about Tom's spiritual life, but she couldn't bring herself to ask. She hadn't been a model Christian herself, so she wondered, what right did she have to ask Tom about his spiritual life?

Finally, Tom proposed to her and she accepted. Her mother had asked her about Tom's relationship to Christ, and Linda had told her that he was a Christian even though she honestly didn't know what his thoughts were about all that. They soon married, and through the years it had never been an issue—until now. Her mother's death had changed something in Linda, and now her spiritual life as well as Tom's mattered to her for the first time.

She and Tom had talked about life after death when her mother died. For the first time she asked him about his own spiritual history and his view on the matter of faith in Christ. He told her that he had never given it much thought. He respected her view and her renewed interest in spiritual things, but those issues didn't particularly interest him. He said he was happy with his life the way it was.

In one of our early counseling sessions together, Linda said she believed Tom thought her renewed interest in spiritual matters would subside as she adjusted to her mother's death. But it didn't happen that way. Instead, her desire to live out the faith of her childhood intensified as the days passed.

She began to read her Bible every day. She found a growing hunger to read books written by Christian authors, and when a friend invited her to join a newly formed Bible study, she accepted. She even attended a weekend women's retreat with another friend.

Tom didn't oppose any of this, and Linda was thankful for that. But he didn't particularly support it either. He seemed to have a "live and let live" perspective. This wasn't enough for Linda. She wanted more than that from him.

Did You Make a Mistake?

"I know I should be thankful that Tom isn't against my growing faith," she said. "But I want him to share it with me, and I don't know how that can possibly happen. He's not even a Christian, and he seems to have no interest in all this. I can't help but think that although Tom and I have always loved each other, I might have been wrong to marry him. The Bible does say not to be unequally yoked with an unbeliever, and that's exactly what I did when I married Tom. I knew deep down that he probably wasn't a Christian."

Linda's frustration about her husband is far more common among Christian women than many realize. It's one thing to be married to a man who is a Christian but isn't as enthusiastic about his faith as you might like, but what if you're married to somebody who doesn't even share the core values of your faith? If the foundation of your life is Jesus Christ but a relationship with Him isn't even on your husband's radar, how can God bless your relationship? The Bible plainly says that light can't have communion with darkness, doesn't it?

It's a legitimate question that deserves an answer. If you are married to an unbeliever and you let your mind dwell on the spiritual gulf between you, you are likely to live in apprehension and fear about the possibility of having a spiritually strong marriage. If you let your thoughts wander down that road long enough, you may eventually wonder if you should even be married to your husband. So before we move on to an answer, let me go ahead and tell you plainly. If you've been thinking this way, it's time to stop. Believing the worst about your husband, his spiritual condition, and your future together isn't going to help the matter.

Focus on the Future

The key to moving through this kind of situation is to change your focus. Putting your attention on your husband's spiritual deficits isn't going to take you to a good place in any way. Asking yourself whether your decision to marry him was right or wrong doesn't offer an ounce of help. Even the apostle Paul stressed the importance of looking ahead and not behind. "I do not regard myself as having laid hold of it yet; but one thing I do: forgetting what lies behind and reaching forward to what lies ahead, I press on toward the goal" (Philippians 3:13-14).

Nobody would suggest that the best scenario is for a believer and unbeliever to marry each other, but there's no benefit in going back now and reliving the past. We're not talking about *premarital* advice here. We're talking about a marriage that has already happened. The relevant question isn't what you should have done. The question is, what do you do now? So stay focused on the right question.

Our Father has identified Himself by name. He's the I AM, not the I WAS. In other words, He is a present-tense God who will work in your situation right now, regardless of what has happened in your past. So your first step is to stop living in the past by focusing on what you should or shouldn't have done. It's done now and it is what it is, so don't torment yourself by living back there. It will lead nowhere good.

Focus on Your Father

The next step is to put your eyes on your Sovereign God. Set aside biblical questions about believers and unbelievers marrying each other. What does that have to do with you now? Again, it's done, and you couldn't go back in time and do things differently even if you wanted to. What value is there in wallowing in doubts about decisions you've already made? There is no value at all, so don't do it. Instead, focus on your Father and who He is to you.

When you've stopped obsessing on the rightness or wrongness of your decision to marry your husband, you'll be able to focus on the reality of who your Father is and how He figures into this whole situation. As your faith moves you in that direction, you'll find more of the mental and emotional relief you need.

Sometimes we have to stand on some foundational truths in order to find a sense of security. If you ever wonder whether you married the right person, here's an eternal truth that will give you a strong foundation to stand on. Your heavenly Father always has been and always will be sovereign over your life. Nothing you've done or ever will do is outside His supervision or beyond what He allows you to do.

That truth may sound simple, but it is actually very profound and can bring you peace if you'll embrace it. Your Father, who loves you more than He loves His own life, has always had ultimate control over everything you've done, and that includes the decision you made to marry your husband. He could have stopped it, but He didn't, so you can trust that He will work this out for your highest good and His greatest glory. Yes, He allowed you to make your own choice, but He also knew you would find yourself at the place you are today. He knew the time would come when you would have concerns about having married an unbeliever, but He also knew He would be here, in this present moment, to walk you through it and to work out His purpose for your life.

God Is Bigger than Our Bad Choices

What is your Father's purpose for you now? His purpose is for you to trust Him! How could God use "a wrong thing" as if it were "a right thing"? The same question could be asked about many circumstances of biblical characters. Moses killed a man and buried him in the sand. Then he ran to the desert, where he hid for 40 years. In that desert he met God in a burning bush, and that was his first step back to Egypt, where he led Israel out of slavery. Moses learned that God's grace was bigger than his own poor choices.

Joseph's brothers sold him into slavery. Years later, when famine struck their land, they learned that he had become the leader who would save them from starvation. God's goodness was obviously bigger than their badness.

Do you see the point? Many people in the Bible made unwise choices and did wrong things, but they didn't derail God's plan. He's bigger than our choices.

Maybe the cross of Jesus Christ is the best example of all. Was it right for evil men to crucify Jesus? Not at all, but again we see how our God stands above all human decisions and redeems them for His glory. He transformed their wrong actions at the cross into the *best* thing humanity will ever know or experience for all eternity. So if He could turn something that evil—the crucifixion of His own Son—into something good, do you really think that if you married an unbeliever, His hands are tied behind His back and that He can't work in your marriage to accomplish something good?

It's important to understand this next statement: Your God stands above right and wrong and holds all of life in His hands. If you allow yourself to be trapped in dualism, believing that right choices allow God to accomplish His intended purposes but that wrong choices tie His hands, you are setting yourself up for pain. Our God stands tall over *all*—both good and evil.

God prohibits some things because they can hurt us, and He doesn't want that to happen. Perhaps you've already learned that if you're married to a man who doesn't share your faith. However, your choice hasn't wounded God or stolen His ability to do what He wants to do. You married an unbeliever? Okay, is that a problem that's too big for your God to handle?

Redemption, Not Retribution

If your marriage isn't what you want it to be, don't allow yourself to think that God is somehow punishing you for making a wrong choice. That isn't how the God of grace operates. Your Father's heart is to redeem your situation. His intention is always toward redemption, not retribution. You aren't being punished, so don't let that thought even begin to creep into your mind.

Remember this too: God loves your husband as much as He loves you. Christ died for your husband as much as He did for you. He doesn't see you as inside His loving grace and your unbelieving husband as outside His loving grace. You can be assured that God is working even now to reveal Himself to your husband. So don't punish yourself now for a decision you made in the past. Instead, love your husband as he is right now and then relax and watch God work.

As a reminder, I'm not writing now about the wisdom or biblical teaching concerning whether a single person following Jesus is to marry an unbeliever. I'm writing to help the person who has already entered that marriage. The best advice I can offer you is this: Stop analyzing the whole thing, stop worrying about whether you've missed the chance to enjoy a blessed marriage, stop thinking negative things about your future, and put your hope in the One who loves you and your husband more than anybody ever has or ever will.

The Bible says that God wrote out your diary and filled in your calendar before you lived a single second of them (see Psalm 139:16). Setting aside the question of whether He decreed your actions or simply wrote what He saw in advance, the fact remains that nothing in your life ever catches Him by surprise. He knew every event before any of them happened, and that certainly includes whom you married. So if your Father knew your decision in advance and He has permitted it, you can be sure that He isn't biting His fingernails right now, worrying that you might have set in motion a dismal future that He can do nothing about. He has everything under control. He always has. You don't have to live with fears and doubts about your past, your present, or your future.

You can be assured that you are with the man your Father wants you to be with. You can trust that God's Spirit is more interested in your husband's spiritual fulfillment than even you could be and that He certainly isn't going to give up on him.

The bottom line is that you can relax and know that your life and marriage aren't stumbling along in a helter-skelter sort of way. The Divine Architect has everything under control, and He will see that it all comes together according to His plan and His schedule.

Be Yourself

How are you to live with an unbeliever? The answer is simple, if not always easy. Just be yourself. Allow your growing faith in Christ to be as much a normal part of your words and actions as everything else in life. Don't try to act spiritual. That's often a religious, manipulative technique wives use, and it won't work. You *are* spiritual, so just relax and be yourself.

The Bible gives you special hope: "Your godly lives will speak to them without any words. They will be won over by watching your pure and reverent lives" (1 Peter 3:1-2 NLT). So don't fall for the idea that you have to convince your husband to trust Christ. That's the Holy Spirit's job. As your husband sees Christ in you, your life will serve as salt to make him thirsty for Christ and light to show him the way. Talk about Christ when God obviously arranges a "divine moment," but don't take on the burden of thinking you're responsible to convince your husband to trust Christ. That duty belongs to somebody else, and He isn't panicking about the matter.

4

Intrinsic Value

"He makes me feel like nothing more than a maid some-times," Erika said to me as she pointed at her husband, Frank. We were at a couples retreat where I was the speaker, and apparently the teaching I'd done about experiencing an intimate relationship in marriage had opened wounds among some of the people there, including Erika.

As we talked together, I quickly saw that Erika's story was like many I've heard from wives who want more from their marriage relationship than they're experiencing right now. Like many wives, Erika felt frustrated and even angry at times because her husband didn't seem to value her.

I've heard variations of her complaint many times. "He makes me feel like I'm just a maid." "He makes me feel like I'm just his personal assistant." "He makes me feel like a nobody." I've even heard more than a few wives say, "He makes me feel like a prostitute." The common denominator in each of these complaints is that according to the wives, the husbands make them feel as if they don't have much value.

Affirmation and Value

If you feel badly about yourself because of the way your husband treats you, two things are important to understand. I'll state the most obvious first: To desire affirmation from your husband is normal. God's plan is for your husband to express loving affirmation to you. As Christ expresses His life through him, your husband will value and affirm you.

It's not wrong for you to want that. For you to want to feel valued by your husband is completely normal. You wouldn't be normal if you didn't want it. All of us want to know that our mates see great value in us, and we hunger to have them express that fact through their words and their actions.

The second thing about your desire to feel valued might be more challenging for you to accept, but it's true nonetheless. It's this: Looking to your husband to validate your personal value is a misguided action. God didn't create you to find your value in your husband. Your value comes from your God, not your mate.

Don't misunderstand what I'm suggesting. If your husband were acting the way the Father would have him behave, he would be doing the things that let you know how much he values you. If he were depending on Christ within him to animate his actions in this area, he most certainly would be affirming you. He would speak and act in a way that would cause you to feel loved and appreciated and valued. The problem is that you can't make that happen. Only God can, so you'll need to determine what you're going to do until that time comes.

Through the years I've had wives come to me for counseling and explain that their problem was the way their husbands behaved. I've often responded by saying, "Well, I'm sorry to disappoint you, but I can't help him because he's not here. The only one I can help right now is you." The same is true regarding your sense of personal worth and value. If I were writing this book for your husband, I would have plenty to say to him about this topic. But the book isn't written for him, and he's not the one reading it. It's directed to you, so there's no benefit in discussing what he might or might not do to improve the situation.

You're the one who needs to understand this situation and know how to act in the midst of it, so my words will be about you and for you. Trust your Father to work in your husband. But in the meantime, it's important to sort out this matter from a biblical perspective. Your goal is to understand that your value doesn't depend on any man, but on your Creator, who made and adores you.

The Heart of the Matter

Remember that Erika said, "He makes me feel…" Embedded in that claim is the heart of the problem. The truth is that Frank didn't make her feel anything. Erika's feelings of low self-esteem were the result of underlying insecurities that were already in her. Frank's behavior just pushed the emotional and mental buttons that activated those feelings. Frank didn't cause Erika to feel the way she did. Her own lack of knowledge about her true value caused those negative feelings to rise up in her. If Erika truly knew who she was, nobody—not even her husband—could rob her of that assurance.

Frank probably needed to change his behavior toward Erika. But more importantly, Erika needed to change the way she saw herself with or without Frank's validation. The most important thing she needed wasn't for Frank to see her differently. It was for her to see herself differently based on an accurate understanding of how *God* sees her. There's the catalyst for transformation in her life.

Anytime our own sense of self-worth depends on the opinion of other human beings, we put ourselves in a no-win situation. If we empower others to determine our value, we will inevitably spend our energy trying to adjust our behavior so they will give us the acceptance we long for. When the way you feel about yourself depends on somebody else's verdict, even if that person is your mate, you're in a bad situation. Nobody but God should have that much power over us. To give others that much power will imprison us in a performance-based lifestyle. We will forever try to do things that will get their approving nod. To say the least, it's an exhausting way to live.

Have you fallen into this trap in your marriage? To find out, ask yourself whether the following description is true about you. You try to do things in a way that will cause your husband to affirm your value. When you do well, he affirms you, and you feel healthy and whole. When he doesn't affirm you, or even worse, when he criticizes you, you feel like a failure. You renew your determination to try harder next time so you'll feel valued again.

Does that describe you? If so, let me put this plainly: That has to change. You're going to become an exhausted, worn-out old woman down the road if you don't trust the Lord to guide you into a better approach.

God's Precious Possession

Your value as a person is inseparably joined to your identity in Jesus Christ. He has given you incredible value by choosing you to be His own precious possession. You are valuable because He chose you.

The divine lover of the universe determined that He wants you to be His bride for all eternity. He left heaven and came to earth in search of you. He found you, and by His finished work at the cross, He swept you up into His embrace and sat with you in His arms in the group hug of the Father, Son, and Holy Spirit. He is never going to let you go. You are precious to Him and always will be.

Your husband's verdict about you does not give you value. Your God's verdict about you does that. It's important for you to see this reality so that you can begin to rest in your true identity and stop trying to build one by the way you act. The Bible teaches that you are a masterpiece, created by the hand of God Himself. You bear His very image and possess His nature. Nothing is wrong with you. You may not always think the right way or act the right way or feel as if nothing is wrong with you, but those things don't define you. Your Creator defines you, and He has declared that you are perfect to Him and for Him. So don't empower your husband with an authority that belongs only to God.

Believe what your heavenly Father says about you. When you do, you will grow in self-respect and will begin to project a God-given assurance and dignity that will command respect from other people. Others usually won't respect you more than you respect yourself. It's up to you to teach people, including your husband, how to see you and how to treat you. That will happen only when you gain an accurate understanding of your true value.

God's Appraisal of You

I'm not suggesting that you muster a good self-image by convincing yourself that you have value. I'm saying that you need a *biblical* self-image—one based on the way God sees you. Whatever He says about your value is true regardless of what your friends, your husband, or even you may think about the matter. God makes that call because nobody else is qualified to do so.

What does He say about the person you are? He says you are the work of His own hands. He says you are pure. He says you are righteous and holy. He says you are beloved and special to Him. He says you are an example to the whole world of what a person can be when she lives out of His grace. Read the New Testament for yourself, and you'll see that the Scripture is filled with affirmations of your value.

Imagine finding a ring in a parking lot. The ring has a stone in it that looks like a one-karat diamond, but you don't really know if the stone is real. Of course, you immediately wonder about its value. How will you find out its worth?

You could take it to various people and ask their opinions. One would say it looks like cubic zirconium and is probably worth only $200. Somebody else might tell you she thinks it's a real diamond and is worth $5000 or more. Another person could say, "Are you kidding? It's *plastic*!" His view would be that it isn't worth $20. How would you find out the true value? You would take it to a professional appraiser, and he would determine its value based on what most buyers would be willing to pay for it on the open market. If somebody were willing to pay $5000 for the ring, it would be accurate to say that its value was $5000.

When it comes to knowing your own value, the same application can be made. If you aren't sure of your true worth, you may tend to get opinions from other people and draw conclusions about your value based on their responses. Maybe you've assessed your value according to what you think your husband's appraisal of your worth is.

The fact is that the only way you can know your real value is to trust the Expert to reveal your worth. That Expert is your heavenly Father. He appraises your value in the same way the jeweler appraises the ring—based on what somebody is willing to pay for you. That's not hard for Him to know because He bought you Himself. "You were bought with a price," and the price paid for you was Jesus Christ Himself (1 Corinthians 7:23).

That means you are as valuable as the Son of God. That is your true worth regardless of whether you, your husband, or anybody else thinks so. It's true because God says so, and that settles the matter. Do you feel as if your value isn't much? If so, you're wrong. Your value is great.

Commanding Respect

Could there be a connection between the way you believe your husband values you and the way you see yourself? I find that is often the case with wives I counsel. You may be surprised that as you come to know and accept the value God bestowed on you, you will experience a growing sense of confidence about who you are. When that happens in a woman, her husband often sees her personal development and begins to value her more.

You've noticed that certain people command respect. They seem to exude a sense that they are worthy of high esteem and admiration. As you grow in your belief about your value in Jesus Christ, you will unconsciously exude that belief. Your husband will see more than self-confidence in you. He will see what might be called "Christ confidence" because your esteem will be based on your authentic identity in Him.

It's important to your marriage for you to know and believe this so you won't be held hostage by what other people do or don't do. In fairness to your husband, he should not be expected to give you your sense of value. That's not his role, and for you to impose such a heavy responsibility on him isn't fair to him. It's also not fair to you because you'll never feel the weight of your true value as long as you look to him to provide it for you. And last but certainly not least, it doesn't honor your Father in heaven for you to need a second opinion about your value, as if what He says isn't enough to convince you.

You are a precious treasure. That's not empty flattery intended to make you feel better about yourself. It's an objective fact that can free you from a never-ending and futile attempt to feel good about yourself by milking affirmation from other people through your actions. My first book, *Grace Walk*, addresses our identity in Christ. If your image of yourself is different from my description of the way God sees you, this is an area where you need to grow. Trying to gain a greater sense of self-worth from another person is like drinking salt water when you're thirsty. It won't work. Only the Water of Life Himself can quench your thirst to know and feel your true value.

5

Bible Bangers

Daniel came home from work one day in a sullen mood. Ellen thought that he probably had another bad day and that he would feel better after dinner. This sort of thing had been happening often. When she told him dinner was ready, Daniel said he wasn't hungry and sat in his home office in front of the computer.

By the time Ellen had fed the children and loaded the dishwasher, he still hadn't come out of his office. She stepped inside and asked, "Is everything okay?" He said nothing, but the expression on his face told her in no uncertain terms that things were not okay—not at all.

"Daniel, what's wrong?" she asked.

"We need to talk, Ellen." She would never forget the moment he made that statement. The talk that followed brought an irrevocable change to her life. Daniel wanted to talk about a divorce.

Ellen and I met together only four months after the divorce to discuss her life. "The bottom line is that this divorce was caused by my faith in Christ and nothing else," she said. "I lived a godly lifestyle the whole time Daniel and I were married, and I always encouraged him to do the same. I know divorce is wrong in the sight of God, but I had no control over this. This whole thing was his fault. I know I'm not perfect, but I see this as nothing other than my suffering for righteousness' sake."

I heard the words Ellen spoke, and I knew she was sincere, but something about what she said and the way she said it left me feeling uneasy. Something about her demeanor bothered me. At first I couldn't put my finger on what it was, but in the weeks ahead it became clear to me.

"Oversaved"

Ellen is a sincere Christian lady, but she expresses her faith through her religious zeal more than she does through her loving relationship to Christ. Have you met people like that? Christians on religious steroids? Comedian Michael Jr. says these people are "oversaved." They have definite opinions of what a Christian is supposed to look like, act like, and talk like, and you get the sense that you're being judged if you don't meet their expectations. That was Ellen.

As we talked over a period of time, I gently began to question Ellen about how she and Daniel related to each other about their faith. Her verdict on her ex-husband was immediate and terse. "He is only a nominal Christian."

"Tell me more about that," I said.

"Well, he didn't go to church with me on Sunday night, for starters," she answered. "In fact, if there was something he'd rather do on Sunday morning, he didn't even mind missing then. And whenever I tried to talk to him about spiritual things, he clearly wasn't interested."

"What kind of spiritual things?" I asked.

"A lot of things," Ellen answered. "Spiritual warfare, the signs of the times in prophecy, things we had going on in our church…I tried to talk about a lot of things, but he just wasn't interested."

"Do you think he really wasn't interested in his relationship to

Christ, or do you think he just didn't particularly enjoy discussing those topics?" I asked.

I could see that my question irritated Ellen. "If a man loves God, won't he want to talk about the things of God?" She clearly thought I should know better.

In all the time I spent with Ellen, I never did feel as if I was able to give her the help she needed. She stopped coming for her counseling appointments after I tried to talk to her about the different ways Christians experience and express their faith. It was apparent to her that there should be no differences.

Matching the Template

Ellen's attitude toward Daniel was more damaging than she realized. Some wives have a mental picture of what a truly spiritual husband should be like, and these women won't be satisfied unless their husbands evolve into that kind of person. Their template of "the godly husband" leaves no room for any variation.

Understanding this fact about your husband's spiritual life can save you a lot of headache and heartache: *A man doesn't have to look religious to be a godly husband.* Remember that religious people criticized Jesus Christ Himself because He didn't act the way their religion required Him to behave. Faith isn't about acting religious. The lifestyle of a Christian is about possessing and expressing the indwelling life of Jesus Christ, and that looks unique in each of us.

I know a man who doesn't attend church with his wife, and it bothers her. I've known the couple for many years. He is a Christian man who has integrity. He acts lovingly toward everybody. I've never heard him say a critical remark about anybody. I've seen him make sacrifices to help people in need. He's a mild-mannered man, and I can't imagine him boldly trying to convince somebody else to trust in Jesus Christ, but his gentle, loving demeanor is a clear expression of Christ. He has many friends who also are believers, and he sees them often. I've discussed his faith in Christ with him many times, and his is a heartwarming story of grace and faith.

I also know the church his wife attends. The congregation has a long history of division and strife. I know the weekday lifestyles of some of the key leaders there, and they aren't the kind of lifestyles that honor Christ. I know the gossip, the judgmental attitude, and the sectarian arrogance of that congregation. I hope he never goes to that church with her. I'm afraid it might ruin him.

God's Voice and Your Voice

You may be thinking, "But my church isn't like that!" Okay, maybe your husband could benefit from being with your church friends, but it's not up to you to make that happen. Let God work in his life. Your husband has a reason for doing the things he does and not doing other things. Will you entrust him and all those things to God? At the risk of sounding too harsh, is it possible that he can't hear God's voice because of the constancy of your voice?

If this line of reasoning causes you to feel anger, consider asking yourself why. Is the previous paragraph untrue or unbiblical? Wouldn't it apply to *some* people? If you've tried your best to convince your husband to do what you think he should do and it's not working, isn't it possible that you need to resign from your campaign and see what God might do apart from your efforts?

I've used the example of going to church because that seems to be the most common complaint I hear from wives about what their husbands won't do. (The second is that they don't read their Bibles enough.) Christians may do many activities, but those actions are to flow out of the life of Christ, who dwells in us. If those activities are pumped up and out into behavioral change, they amount to nothing more than dead religious activity. I know you want more from your husband than rote religious routine. With that in mind, I offer this as graciously and yet as plainly as I know how: Stop taking on the role of God's Spirit in your husband's life. Let the Holy Spirit create hunger in him in His time and in His way.

External Expectations and Internal Motivation

I realize that you already know there's a big difference between being religious and being a Christian, but many wives who know that *still* want their husbands to act religious. They have a job description in their minds of what their husbands should look like, and they set out to shape their man into that person. Because of your own church background or family upbringing, you may have formulated a mental picture of what he will look like when he grows spiritually into the man you've prayed for him to become.

This chapter isn't about a man who has no interest in spiritual things or no personal walk of faith. I'm writing here about husbands who profess faith in Christ but don't meet their wives' expectations of what a believer should look like.

Have you had a particular expectation of what your husband's spiritual walk needs to be like? Have you subtly or sometimes not so subtly tried to nudge him in that direction? If so, you may sincerely believe you're doing a good thing, but you're not. If your husband is going to live as the godly person his heavenly Father wants him to be, you're going to need to let God be the One who decides how it is going to look. Your Father can do a much better job of shaping your husband into the man He has created him to be than you can.

The fact is that trying to impose expectations of your husband's spiritual growth is legalistic. That may sound harsh, but it's true. Legalism focuses on outward behavioral change as a means for advancing spiritually. Grace internally motivates a person toward a deeper acceptance of the love of God until that very love becomes the transforming agent in his life. A wife doesn't have the ability to place internal motivation within her husband. Only the Holy Spirit can do that, and He is quite capable and eager to do it!

Legalism and Grace

Legalism commands a duty to be fulfilled. Grace creates a desire to be followed. Legalism stands on responsibility. Grace stems from relationship. Legalism is about religious conformity to standards of behavior. Grace is about a righteous commitment to being our real selves.

Look at the contrasts between legalism and grace in the previous paragraph. Which approach do you take in your own life? Which do you want your husband to take? There is a stark difference between the two approaches, and they will lead to very different outcomes.

Maybe your husband indeed does need to grow spiritually. Maybe he does need to have a deeper interest in his walk with Christ. It's important for you to fully understand that the solution to that need is *not* for his behavior to change in some way. It's not up to you to presume to guide, advise, coerce, or manipulate him into doing what you think he needs to be doing. Once again, for emphasis: Only the Holy Spirit can be the solution to what he needs. For you to try to manage the situation by solving his problem can actually interfere with and impede what God's Spirit is doing in him.

Ellen seemed to think that God needed her help. She kept trying to change her husband until he decided he couldn't stand it anymore. She told me that one day Daniel said to her, "I've tried to be a good husband. I've been a good provider. I've always supported you in anything you wanted to do. But no matter what I do, it's never enough for you. I've tried, Ellen, but I'm tired of trying." So he walked.

This is a typical reaction to legalistic heavy-handedness. The Bible teaches that legalism ministers death and condemnation to people, and that's exactly what Ellen's approach did to Daniel. It caused him to feel as if he could never measure up, so he finally gave up. Imposing spiritual expectations on your husband is not the way of grace. Loving is the way of grace. Affirmation of authentic spiritual progress is the grace way. Acceptance and patience and quiet hope and prayer are the ways of grace.

You likely want to see your husband change. You probably want it badly, but don't let your desire for God to work in his life cause you to become impatient and try to move things along by taking the situation into your own hands. Your Father knows what He is doing, so let Him do it.

Any attempt to change your husband is a misguided effort regardless of how sincere you might be. Trying to change him communicates that he isn't meeting your expectations and that he will not be acceptable to you until he improves his behavior. Is that what you want to communicate? I know it isn't.

Accepting Him As He Is

Did you know that God accepts and loves your husband right where he is today? If he is a believer who shows little interest in God right now, God still loves him. Even if he's not a believer, your Father still loves him. Wherever your husband is in his spiritual walk, God accepts him where he is and as he is.

Do you believe that? I hope so because it's true. God isn't waiting for your husband to change before He will accept him. Are you convinced that's true? If so, why would you impose a higher standard on your husband than God Himself does? Instead, why not show your husband the same unconditional love and acceptance that his Father does and accept him where he is right now?

If you are trying to change your husband, it's important for you to see that your attempt is legalistic, futile, and very much unlike the way your heavenly Father relates to him. I know I have repeated several times the importance of not trying to change your husband. It's not accidental. I repeat myself here because I've seen how common this problem is.

Just love him, accept him, and pray for him. Change will come, but it will be delayed if you wrongly believe you're the one who can make it happen. The One who knows what it takes to change him is the One who created him and who loves him more deeply than even you ever could. So entrust your husband to Him and know that He isn't going to give up until the job is done.

6

Soured Saints

After Abby and Ted were married in their midtwenties, their lifestyle looked much like that of their Christian friends and family. Their faith was an integral part of their lives. They took their two children, Sarah and Benji, to Sunday school every week because they wanted them to learn the Bible stories that Abby and Ted had learned as children. The kids loved going to church and participating in the children's church services, where the children's pastor continually came up with innovative and interesting ways to teach them.

Life seemed to be going smoothly until their son, Benji, began to feel fatigued much of the time. He also seemed to bruise very easily and often had a bloody nose that was hard to stop. When Abby and Ted took Benji to his pediatrician, they weren't prepared for what they would hear. The diagnosis was leukemia.

They were both stunned by the diagnosis but determined to beat it. As time progressed, Benji's white blood-cell count continued to increase while his red blood cells diminished. Eventually, it became apparent that he wasn't going to survive this ordeal.

On a cold Saturday morning in October, Ted and Abby sat beside Benji's bedside as he quietly breathed his last breath. He was buried in the family cemetery in Ted and Abby's hometown. The day Benji died, something also died inside Ted.

Over the months that followed Benji's death, Abby moved through the normal grief process. She was depressed and stayed home alone most of the time in the beginning. She dealt with the anger and the depression in a way that most people would. Although tears would still come to her eyes when she talked about Benji, she eventually began to attend worship services at her church again and even met her girlfriends for lunch regularly. Little by little, her life-style began to be normal again.

Ted's experience was different from Abby's. Rather than move through the stages of grief, he seemed to sour emotionally. From the moment Benji died, he drew into himself and said very little about the experience. Abby tried to talk to him and encourage him, but Ted was unresponsive to anything she said.

Finally, one day Abby asked Ted if they could pray together about the pain he was feeling. At that moment, all the emotion Ted had suppressed came pouring out as rage. "Pray about *what*?" he shouted. "The time for praying was six months ago when my son died, and it didn't do a bit of good!" For what seemed like forever to Abby, he raged. The incident ended when he finally turned and stormed out of the room.

Later, when Abby tried to bring up the subject again, Ted looked calmly into her eyes and said, "Abby, I'm sorry for venting my anger like that. It was wrong for me to unleash on you, but you need to know something. I'm done with faith. I'm done with prayer. I'm done with church. I'm done with it all."

Abby knew better than to try reasoning with him. The resolute way he spoke caused her to know he meant it. "Okay, Ted," she meekly answered. Then she walked out of the den and into her bedroom, where she quietly cried.

I met Abby at a conference where I spoke one weekend. She asked me if she could speak to me after the last session, and I agreed.

As we met together, she shared with me how hard her life had been in the past year since the blowup with Ted. "I want to live out my faith, but I don't know how to do this alone," she said. "Ted and I always shared this part of our lives, and now I feel alone. He doesn't criticize me about my faith as long as I say nothing to him about it, but if I try to say even one word to encourage him, he becomes sullen and walks out of the room."

Abby and Ted's situation certainly isn't unique, but it isn't something that most couples face. Thankfully, most of us know nothing of burying one of our children. But many wives do know the experience of being married to a man who wants nothing to do with faith and even takes a belligerent stand toward spiritual matters. I've talked to countless women whose husbands, for one reason or another, have little patience with their expression of faith in Christ.

What's a woman to do when her husband is antagonistic toward her spiritual walk? How is she to live out her faith in a meaningful way at home when it agitates her husband and perhaps even causes conflict? Is she to tone it down for him? Or is she to act boldly so that she doesn't compromise her faith? Is there a balance between the two?

The answers to these questions are complex. Don't let anybody tell you the solution is simple. If you're in this kind of situation, well-meaning friends or family may give you answers about how you should live at home, but those people aren't in your shoes. Simplistic answers come easily for those who don't know what you're facing. Real life, however, seldom cooperates with simplistic solutions.

Give Yourself a Break

Is your husband antagonistic toward your faith? If so, I'll begin my remarks to you by commending you. You are indeed an exemplary woman of faith because of your commitment and determination to live out your relationship to Christ in such a challenging environment.

You may not feel as if you're a very good Christian at times. I'd be surprised if it were otherwise. After all, your emotions are constantly battered as you try to walk the fine line between expressing your faith and not agitating your husband. Your mind often spins, trying to understand what behavior is right and what should be avoided for the sake of peace at home. It's a tough place to be in, and anyone in your situation would sometimes feel as if she wasn't doing a good job. You are to be commended for your spiritual commitment and your desire to live out your walk with Christ. That speaks volumes of positive things about you and about the Christ who indwells you.

The first thing you need to know and accept is that no wife in your situation handles it perfectly all the time. It's normal for you to feel anger toward your husband at times. It's also normal if you don't always respond to him the way you think a perfect Christian should. It's even normal for resentment to try to take root in you at times.

So give yourself a break by not dwelling on the times and ways you don't handle things with a godly, flawless execution. You're going to blow it sometimes. When you do, show yourself grace by not dwelling on your mistakes. Put them behind you, get up, and go forward again as you trust God's Spirit to lead you. Put out any fire you started in an impulsive moment. If needed, apologize. Forgive yourself for not being perfect. Put your eyes on Christ and move on. Dwelling on the less-than-perfect way you might have reacted to your husband is going to dig a trench of self-condemnation that will become harder to escape the longer you dig it. So don't do that. Don't even let yourself go there for a moment. When you mess up, do your best to get up, look up to Him, straighten up your actions, and keep going forward with Christ.

Whose Problem Is It?

If your husband is antagonistic toward your faith, a second important thing for you to clearly recognize is that the problem is his, not yours. I don't mean to suggest that you shouldn't care about your husband's spiritual condition. Of course you will care for him and pray for him, but you can't solve the problem. That's important to remember.

I've seen wives take on the duty of becoming pastor, counselor, teacher, life coach, psychologist, and psychiatrist to their husbands, and it always ends the same way—in mental and emotional burnout. Make yourself available to your husband if he invites your help in processing through his anger, but it is unwise for you to unilaterally assume that role. Your sincere effort may do more harm than good.

You may have noticed that in every chapter, I have stressed that you can't change your husband. There's a reason I keep reiterating that point. It's because *you can't change your husband.* We need to repeatedly emphasize this lesson because most people don't learn it easily. I've heard wives as well as husbands say, "Yes, I know I can't change my mate," and then turn right around and try to change their spouse. It's a futile attempt that will do nothing other than annoy your husband and frustrate you.

Your husband's spiritual issue is between his Father and himself. Because you love your husband, you want to see a spiritual transformation come to him *now.* It sometimes seems as if we live our lives with a stopwatch in hand while God approaches our lives with a calendar in His hand. That fact can be very frustrating at times, but we aren't going to rush the work of God regardless of what we do.

Let go of the idea that there must be *something* you can do to reach your husband. There isn't, and if you don't know that, you run the risk of interfering with what the Holy Spirit may be doing in your husband's life. Sometimes the best thing we can do is to entrust the one we love to our Father and then get out of the way.

Meaning Well but Not Helping

An incident in Scripture illustrates this. Jesus was telling His disciples that He was going to go to Jerusalem, where He would be offered up and die on the cross. When Peter heard Him say this, he cried out, "Never, Lord! This shall never happen to You!"

We can all understand how Peter must have felt at that moment. He loved Jesus and didn't want to see Him hurt. But Peter didn't realize that for Jesus to go to the cross was the Father's plan for Him. The Father Himself was moving Jesus closer to His crucifixion.

Peter stood between Jesus and the cross. He tried to help Jesus by preventing the crucifixion from happening, but he was actually standing between Jesus and the Father's will for Him. Peter meant well. He thought he was helping, but he wasn't. He was interfering.

Can you see how the same thing could apply to what God is doing in your husband's life? Your attempts to help alleviate his pain may actually be counterproductive. Our Father may be using the pain in his life. Of course you will show love to your husband, but leave it up to God to bring him through the underlying pain he feels. His antagonism about faith stems from pain, and only God can heal that.

Anger and Pain

Recognizing this fact can help immeasurably. Anger isn't your husband's root problem. That's only the symptom. Anger about spiritual things is the result of hurts that lie beneath the surface. Showing anger is often easier than showing hurt, especially for men. As you see your husband's anger flair up at times, remind yourself that you're really seeing an expression of pain. Men often unconsciously and mistakenly believe that showing pain is an expression of weakness but that showing anger is an expression of strength. That's why a man who has been hurt will often react in anger. Seeing your husband's anger in that light will help you to respond in grace.

If he says negative things about God, even if they sound horrible to you, don't jump in to defend God. Your husband is simply venting, and that's not necessarily a bad thing. Although it's painful for you to hear, remind yourself that when he vents, at least the poison won't stay inside him, souring his feelings and thoughts even more.

Your Father isn't intimidated when people say foolish things, and He doesn't think you're compromising if you don't come to His defense. He is capable of defending Himself. Have you considered that you may help your husband more by validating his feelings than by trying to talk him out of them?

Rather than scolding him for what he says, consider what you might accomplish by saying something like this: "I know you're upset. You feel that God let us down. It's okay." An affirmation of his feelings as simple as that could possibly open the door to his heart just a little more so that, in due time, he may let you in and talk to you about what he feels.

Here's the rule of thumb to remember when your husband vents his pain through anger. As much as possible, validate his feelings even if you can't agree with his words. "I can understand why you feel that way." That doesn't mean you agree with him. It simply acknowledges that you recognize his feelings. That small ministry of empathy in a moment of crisis can have more healing power than you might imagine.

Your husband's anger doesn't offend God. Our heavenly Father is gracious and kind toward us even when we misbehave. If you could see your husband through God's eyes of agape, you would see that God views him as a wounded child who needs to be tenderly nurtured. He doesn't see him as a rebellious man who needs to be punished if he doesn't get his act together.

Any husband who is belligerent toward his wife's faith is a hurting man. His anger is actually a cry for help that he feels he hasn't yet received. Seeing him that way will soften your own heart and empower you to relate to him with the compassion of Christ.

Unholy Ghosts

*B*efore Brandi and Ethan became followers of Christ, their lifestyle was less than straightlaced. Well, that's putting it mildly. Actually, they both would have called themselves party animals. Their circle of friends enjoyed the same hedonistic lifestyle. It wasn't unusual for Brandi and Ethan to be out until the early morning hours with these friends every weekend. Ethan joked that his favorite things in life were the three *P*s—pot, porn, and partying. Brandi had no problem with that.

Brandi worked out at a gym near her home. There she met Fran, and the two became friends. Brandi immediately liked Fran because of her sincere smile and outgoing personality. The two of them commonly had lunch together after their spinning class at the gym. As the months passed, their friendship continued to develop.

Brandi knew Fran was a Christian, but she appreciated that Fran didn't act particularly religious. Now and then, Fran would say a word that Brandi hadn't heard a Christian say before. Not something really bad, but the sort of thing that the churchy people Brandi had known would never say. To put it another way, Fran just seemed authentic.

Brandi was surprised to find out one day that Fran didn't even attend church. She said she met with a small group in her home once a week but that she'd stopped going to church five years ago. Brandi found that puzzling. She hadn't known a religious person who didn't go to church. Then again, that was the point. Fran wasn't religious, but she was obviously a committed follower of Jesus Christ. The contrast between the two was something Brandi found both refreshing and appealing.

One day at lunch, Fran suggested that she and Brandi and their husbands go to a movie and dinner together. The next week, they saw a movie and then went to Olive Garden. Ethan liked Fran's husband, Tom, a fact that Brandi was happy to see. Over the next few months, the two couples spent many Friday nights together.

One night, Tom told Ethan about the small group that met at his house, and he invited Ethan and Brandi over the next Saturday evening. They went the next week and met other couples that they soon realized all shared a passion about Jesus Christ. Yet like Tom and Fran, these people didn't cause them to feel put off. The people in the group didn't use a lot of religious language, and they seemed accepting of everybody. Ethan's mother had taught him as a child that it was a sin not to pray and give thanks before a meal, but this group just dived right into the spread of Chinese food on the kitchen counter. The group laughed and teased each other. They didn't act socially uptight but seemed relaxed when they were together.

Ethan and Brandi enjoyed these new friends, and over a period of weeks, they found themselves being drawn to the Christ they all knew. One evening, when the group was about to pray together, Tom asked if anybody had anything they wanted to share. Ethan spoke up. "I just want to say that I appreciate the openness I've seen in this group. You guys are the kind of Christian I want to be. I have decided to follow Jesus Christ too, and I want to thank you for helping me come to this place."

"All right!"

"That's great!"

"Cool!" The responses spontaneously echoed from most of the people in the room.

"Me too," Brandi said. "Ethan and I are tracking together on this. I want to follow Jesus too." Fran was sitting beside Brandi and beamed with delight.

The evening couldn't have gone any better. Everybody hugged Ethan and Brandi and encouraged them as they began their Jesus-journey together. The next week Tom baptized them both in the pool in their backyard.

Over the months that followed, Brandi and Ethan spent much of their free time with their new Christian friends. For a while it seemed to Brandi that life couldn't get any better. They attended the home group meeting every week, and Brandi's relationship to the other women deepened more and more. The guys did things together. One weekend they went on a deep-sea fishing trip together. Sometimes they played a round of golf at the public course in town. Things seemed to be going well.

But as the months passed, Brandi began to get some vibes that something wasn't quite right with Ethan. First, he had begun making excuses for not getting together with the group for their weekly get-togethers. He withdrew from the other men in the group and even began to criticize the people there to Brandi over petty things that had no significance at all.

Brandi encouraged him about getting together with the others time and time again, but it just didn't happen. She tried to give him the benefit of the doubt, but his reasons obviously sounded more and more like excuses with every week that passed. Something was wrong. She knew it.

"What's going on with you?" she finally asked Ethan one evening. "We always have fun with these people, but something has obviously changed with you."

"Nothing is wrong," he answered. "I just want our world to be larger than a handful of people we've only known for a short time."

Brandi's confusion didn't last long after that conversation. One morning after Ethan had gone out to jog, she went into his home office to pay a few bills online. When she sat down, she noticed a few windows had been minimized at the bottom of the screen. Thinking Ethan had probably accidentally walked away without closing them and intending to close them herself, she opened them again.

When she opened the second tab minimized at the bottom of the monitor, she felt panic suddenly rush over her. It opened the home page of a porn site. Her mind raced in every direction, trying to make sense out of what she was seeing. She quickly minimized the page and immediately got up and left the room.

About a half hour later, Ethan walked back into the house to find Brandi sitting on the couch with tears in her eyes. "What's wrong?" he asked.

"I'm scared," she answered.

"Scared of what?"

"Scared of what you're doing again," she continued, as she looked downward.

"I don't understand what you mean," Ethan said.

"I think you do understand what I mean," Brandi answered as she looked him directly in the eyes. "I've just come from the computer."

Ethan's whole countenance changed. "I didn't mean for you to see that," he quietly answered.

"Ethan, the question is, why are *you* seeing that? How does that fit our lives anymore?"

Ethan walked over to the couch and sat down beside her. With calm and measured words, he said, "Brandi, right now I'm not where I've been."

"That makes no sense. What do you mean?" she asked.

"I mean that I'm not mentally where we've been over the past months. There are things about our lives before that I miss," he calmly responded.

"Porn?" Brandi asked incredulously.

"No, it's not the porn," Ethan said. "I miss the fun we used to have."

"But we do have fun, and it's not destructive fun either."

"I know," he said, "but don't you ever miss the old times—the *fun* times we used to have?"

"No," Brandi responded. "I'm glad to be away from all that—the porn, the weed, the whole raunchy lifestyle we lived. I'm glad it's over. Those things are ghosts from my past, and I never want to meet them again."

"Why does it have to be either-or? I'm not saying that we should abandon our new friends, but can't we just be normal people sometimes?" Ethan asked.

"That's not normal!" Brandi answered loudly as she pointed toward the office.

"Well, I think it's normal for a lot of people, and I want to party sometimes—you know, the way we used to. In fact, I ran into Dog and his wife at the post office a few days ago, and they invited us to a party they're having this Saturday night."

"Are you serious?" Brandi asked. "Do you *really* want to go back to all that again?"

"Well, not as an every weekend sort of thing, but from time to time I'd like to get with the guys. They're not bad people. And I'd like it if you wouldn't fight me on this. I'm not trying to pull you down, but c'mon. What's the harm in a little old-fashioned fun now and then?"

In a moment, Brandi had a feeling that her world had just changed. In the weeks ahead, her instincts proved to be right. She went to the weekend party with Ethan. She didn't get stoned, but he did. Still, it wasn't just the porn or the pot that worried Brandi. She saw Ethan's old temperament emerging again—the one she had thought would never return.

The hardest part of the whole thing was that he wanted her to get her head in the same place as his—to think the way he did about it all. For the first time in their lives together, Brandi was not only afraid but also confused. They had always shared the same interests and seemed to move in unison together on everything. But now her desires weren't in sync with his, and even worse, he continually tried to get her to "lighten up and live a little." Brandi was afraid to go back to that lifestyle but also afraid not to—afraid that Ethan would go there without her, something that she believed couldn't possibly lead to a good outcome.

The Way of Grace

What is the answer for a wife in a position like the one Brandi faced? She and Ethan may be extreme examples, but many husbands want their wives to do things that don't fit with their commitment to follow Christ. Is a wife to simply give in so she can keep the peace or even for fear that she might lose her husband if she refuses? If she refuses to go along with her husband's destructive decisions, how is she to communicate that to him without causing further damage to the marriage?

The answer to this challenge is the same as the answer to the other challenges we've seen so far in this book. The solution is grounded in grace, but we need to understand what grace does and does not require of us. In this kind of situation, grace must be clearly understood and applied lest a wife unintentionally makes matters worse.

Grace always leads us to act toward other people in the most loving way. Grace is always constructive and never destructive. It always acts toward others in a way that builds them up and never in a way that tears them down.

Read the previous paragraph again and then answer this question: Would it be constructive or destructive for Brandi to yield to Ethan's pressure in order to keep peace in their marriage? Would agreeing to the course of action Ethan wanted build them both up, or would it tear them down?

The answer is obvious. To return to the hedonistic lifestyle of their past would be destructive. It would tear down many aspects of their lives. So if Brandi is going to act in grace, she cannot agree to return to the old lifestyle that Ethan wants to again embrace.

Being Gracious and Being Agreeable

Here's a very important aspect of grace that is often misunderstood: Grace isn't some sort of "sloppy agape" that agrees with everybody about everything. Sometimes grace requires taking a hard stand—one that is firm, resolved, and unyielding. To love a person sometimes requires taking a stance that he or she will not appreciate or accept. Christ lives through you, and He would never agree to sinning with another person.

Ironically, when we act in grace toward others, sometimes they can accuse us of *not* being gracious. When that happens, they are confusing being gracious with being agreeable. Grace isn't always agreeable.

When the apostle Peter was meeting together with Jews who didn't understand the grace of God, he compromised by adapting to their legalistic standards. When the apostle Paul heard about Peter's compromise, Paul "had to oppose him to his face, for what he did was very wrong" (Galatians 2:11 NLT). Paul, the apostle of grace, opposed Peter face-to-face because Peter was dead wrong.

When a husband wants his wife to do something that is plainly inconsistent with the character of the Christ who lives in us, grace compels and enables her to stand firm in her refusal. One of the most loving things you can do in your marriage relationship is to refuse to nurture destructive behavior in your mate. Grace sometimes responds with an uncompromising "No!"

Whatever you may have been taught about grace, you can know that grace *never* asks you to agree to sinful actions. In Brandi and Ethan's case, it wasn't simply a matter of a few missteps that would be wise to avoid. Ethan's choice reflected a desire to return to a lifestyle that was blatantly destructive.

How to Take a Stand

In your own marriage, it is important to be clear about when to take a strong stand. This chapter isn't about mere preferences that may differ from one married couple to the next. It's not talking about gray areas, such as whether to watch an R-rated movie or have a glass of wine. This chapter is addressing actions that are explicitly defined in Scripture as sin. There may be room for discussion in the gray areas, but there is no room for negotiation when it comes to clearly defined sinful behavior.

How does a wife refuse to follow her husband into sinful choices? Attitude is important. When you must refuse to compromise, you don't have to preach a sermon about why the choice is wrong. Your husband already knows why it is wrong.

Acting angry about the matter isn't helpful either. A calm but firm refusal often has more power than an emotional reaction. Don't give your husband reason to accuse you of being hysterical. Don't *react* impulsively—make a plan of how you will *respond*. Do it with an obvious and deliberate resolve. There's no need to apologize or try to soften your refusal either. Don't act in anger, but don't behave as if you're not sure your response is the right one. Be assured as you answer.

The grace of Jesus Christ within you will empower you to navigate through difficult times like these if you should face them. No two situations are exactly the same, so you will need to adapt the guidance in this chapter to fit your own situation. But whenever you are pressured to do something you know would violate who you are in Jesus Christ, the grace of Jesus Christ within you will enable you to respond in a loving yet uncompromising manner. Sometimes saying yes to Christ is to say no to another, even the one you love.

Confronting Bullies

Christie knew when she married Jay that both her mother and her best friend, Jessica, had some concerns. Both of them had questioned her decision because of some things she had told them about Jay. Nothing major, at least in Christie's mind, but they raised red flags for them.

Christie thought they weren't big things, just little quirks in her relationship with Jay. "All relationships have quirky little things that people who love each other have to overlook and be patient about," Christie had reasoned. "I'm not perfect either," she insisted one day when her mother asked her about some of Jay's behavior. Her mother thought it should be taken more seriously than Christie did.

Before they married, Jay was possessive of Christie's time and insisted that she account for practically every minute. Once, she had told him she would be going home after work, but then a friend invited her to have dinner at a nearby restaurant. While she was in the restaurant, Jay called her apartment but reached her voice mail. When he called her cell phone, Christie didn't hear it ring because of the noisy atmosphere in the restaurant. Jay called three times but didn't reach her.

When she arrived home, she heard his message. Obviously

irritated, he simply said, "You didn't do what you said, did you? Where are you? Call me."

When Christie called Jay and explained what had happened, he said she should have told him her plans had changed before she left work. "But we weren't even going to see each other this evening," Christie replied.

"It doesn't matter," Jay answered firmly. "When you tell me something, I expect it to be that way. You can't just go off doing your own thing without me knowing where you are."

That kind of situation concerned Christie's mom and Jessica. If it were a rare incident, it might not be such a notable thing, but Jay often acted that way. That fact worried the two women, who loved Christie so much.

Another time, in a moment of anger, Jay yelled at Christie after she had neglected to stop by and pick up laundry from the cleaners when he had asked her to. "Jay, I planned on picking them up on the way to work tomorrow morning," she answered.

"What were you thinking, Christie?"

"I thought…" Christie tried to respond.

"That's the problem," Jay interrupted. "You thought. Christie, sometimes you *don't* think. That's your problem. When I ask you to do something, you just need to do it and not come up with a better idea."

Despite ongoing encounters like these, Christie and Jay married four years before I met them. As Christie explained the tension in their marriage to me, her voice trembled more and more. "The way he treats me just isn't right," she said. "I'm not perfect, but I would never talk to him the way he talks to me."

"How is that?" I asked.

"Well, for instance, he's called me 'chunky' in front of friends on more than one occasion. I've put on a few pounds over the past three years, but when I tell him that I don't like that, he says that

I'm too sensitive, that it's just a joke. His hairline is receding, but if I were to call him 'baldy,' which I'd never do, there would be a war at our house."

Emotional Abuse

As Christie continued to talk about Jay's behavior, it became increasingly apparent that her husband was mentally and emotionally abusing her. "Has he ever hit you?" I asked.

"No, he would never do that," she responded, obviously needing to defend him. "He's really a good person. I just don't like the way he talks to me."

As Christie and I talked together for almost an hour, it was clear to me that Jay had some serious problems with both his words and his actions toward Christie. He often spoke to her in a demeaning way, using subtle and sometimes not-so-subtle putdowns. He controlled her so much that she couldn't go anywhere or do anything, even for a few hours, without him knowing in advance. If he didn't want her to do something, he challenged her about it. She found herself defending decisions that she shouldn't have needed to explain.

Christie's relationship to her husband is a classic example of being married to a bully. I can't count the number of wives I've counseled through the years whose husbands were verbally and emotionally abusive to them. Most of these women had never been physically struck, but many had no idea how to respond in a healthy way to their husbands' misbehavior.

Maybe your situation is similar to Christie's. Yours might not be as bad, or maybe it's even worse, but one thing is for sure: Your Creator doesn't intend for you to live in an abusive relationship. I'm not suggesting that the relationship should end. If your abuse is physical, that's another issue, and we'll discuss it in chapter 20. In the case of physical abuse, you *must* protect yourself and your children at all costs. However, right now I'm not referring to physical abuse, but to the kind of mistreatment that involves cruel, cutting words and overbearing, controlling behavior.

Some wives think their spiritual duty is to tolerate anything their husbands dish out, but nothing could be further from the truth. You are a person who has great value in God's sight. You belong to Him, and He never wants you to submit yourself to treatment that systematically tears you down and reduces your sense of self-worth.

In chapter 5, we met Ellen, who badgered her husband about his spirituality until he finally walked out on her. In this chapter, Christie's situation is almost the opposite. Her problem isn't that she says too much. It's that she says too little.

Grace divinely empowers us to be all that we've been made to be and do all that we've been made to do. Sometimes God's grace empowers us to shut up, as in Ellen's case. At other times, however, the grace of God empowers us to speak up, such as when a wife is passive in the face of blatant verbal and emotional abuse.

Helping or Hurting?

If your relationship to your husband is anything like the one I've described here, here is an important question to ask yourself. Have you considered that you actually *hurt* your husband when you continue allowing him to act this way? In every marriage, we are always either building each other up or tearing each other down. When your husband says demeaning things to you, he is obviously tearing you down. But did you know that if you allow him to continue to act that way, you are tearing him down too?

How does your passivity hurt him? By allowing him to continue abusing you with his words and overbearing actions, you are implying that his behavior is okay. When you don't speak up for yourself, your silence actually reinforces his poor behavior. Wives and husbands are to encourage, strengthen, and build up each other. Sometimes that requires what author David Augsburger has called "carefrontation," a word that means caring enough to confront somebody.

You may have established a pattern of withdrawal when your husband acts up, but when you withdraw and allow him to continue to misbehave, you aren't helping him, you, or the problem at all. The grace of your Father expressed through the life of Christ's Spirit within you seeks to find a way out of you and into the situation. When you express grace, you can bring healing to the problem. But when you squelch grace inside you, it lies dormant and ineffective.

How to Talk About the Problem

If you've allowed your husband to be abusive so long that it seems normal to you both, this situation may not be changed overnight. However, change can *begin* to take place overnight and continue until your husband relates to you in the proper way—if you are willing to step up in faith and deal with the situation.

How do you do that? It's not complicated, but it will require the kind of courage that you'll find only by relying on Christ within you to empower you. You'll need to discuss the matter with your husband, and afterward, you'll need to insist that he not disrespect you through his words and actions in the future.

Before you talk to him about the situation, it would be very helpful to privately pray for him and yourself. Pray that the Holy Spirit will open his mind and heart to see the truth. Pray that you will know the right moment to discuss the issue with him. Pray that you'll find the best words to express your concerns. Prayer is always the best first step in dealing with any problem.

Then, when the moment comes to speak to your husband about the problem, resolve by Christ's strength to talk to him in a calm but straightforward way. If you become excited, you will only inflame the situation and increase the risk of not being heard over the conflict. Refuse to be drawn into an argument. Your husband may immediately flare up in anger, which is probably a conscious or unconscious attempt to control you by shutting you down. Don't succumb to that. Just continue explaining your concerns calmly.

If he gets loud, respond by getting quieter. If he tries to provoke you to react emotionally, just keep talking calmly. In other words, don't allow him to set the pace or the tone of the conversation by taking it over. You maintain the pace and direction of the conversation by staying focused. He may try to justify his behavior by arguing about a past incident. Don't allow yourself to be pulled off track. Just keep moving forward calmly by explaining your concerns.

A Three-Point Plan

The content of your talk will likely need to include these main points. If it helps you, prepare your thoughts and words by writing them on a pad and keeping that in front of you. Don't risk the chance of becoming emotionally rattled and losing track of the things you intended to say. Here are three main points you'll probably need to discuss in a situation like this.

First, state plainly that you don't appreciate being belittled with demeaning words and that you want it to stop. For instance, when Christie talked to Jay, she could plainly, calmly, but firmly tell him that she does not like to be called chunky and that she doesn't want that to ever happen again. If Jay were to say that she is too sensitive or that he was just joking, she could respond, "Even if you think I am sensitive, I don't want you to talk to me that way anymore," or "You may think it's a joke, but it's not funny to me. It's hurtful and embarrassing, and I want you to stop doing it."

Second, state in clear language that you are not going to sit in silence and allow this type of behavior to continue in the future. But remember this: *You must be willing to follow through* with what you are telling him. He may not believe you're serious about what you're saying until your actions demonstrate that you meant what you said. How can you do that? After this conversation, you must confront him each and every time he repeats his bad habit. If you are inconsistent in responding to him immediately when he lapses, he is not likely to change.

Finally, redefine the way you and your husband relate to each other. Sometimes bad relational habits must be changed in order for that relationship to begin to be healthy. If your husband has been abusive toward you with his words and attitude, don't make excuses for him. He is wrong, and you can't help him until you recognize that fact and admit it to yourself.

However, it is also important for you to recognize and acknowledge your wrong behavior in the situation. "How could I have been wrong? I've been the victim!" you might think. That's true, but you have been the victim only because you've allowed yourself to be the victim. That is where you've been wrong. When people first try to bully others, they are often testing the waters to see how far they can go. If offenses are allowed, the habit is easily established. As it continues, the misbehavior becomes a harmful aspect of an unhealthy relationship.

As you begin asserting yourself by expressing self-respect and refusing to be mistreated, conflict will most likely escalate at first. Abusive husbands have learned to have their way in every situation through heavy-handed control and harsh or critical words. Old habits don't die easily, and your husband may seem to get worse before he gets better. Don't retreat! You must be willing to pay the price to see the needed change come to your relationship. As stated previously, calmly but firmly refuse to be demeaned. Confront the misbehavior every time it happens.

Changing Him or Respecting Yourself?

Having written so much already about how only God can change your husband, am I now contradicting myself? No, I'm not.

Trying to change your husband is different from respecting your-self enough to not allow anybody to habitually disrespect you—not even your husband.

The Bible teaches that we are to love others as we love ourselves. In order to keep that command, we must first love ourselves—not in a narcissistic sort of way that stems from pride, but because we see ourselves as God sees us. It is not prideful or wrong to see the value God has placed on you. In fact, to the contrary, it is important to agree with your Creator and not dispute what He has said about your worth as a person.

Some wives have been so belittled that they can hardly see their true value. If that's true for you, pray and ask the Holy Spirit to show you your true worth. Study Scripture and other resources that will teach and encourage you about your identity in Christ and your Father's love for you. Don't let another person veto God's opinion of you. What He says about you is true regardless of what anyone believes (including you).

As previously stated, grace is the divine enablement for you to be all that you've been made to be and to do all that you've been made to do. You weren't created to be disrespected. To the contrary, your God made you to be loved! Don't show a lack of love for yourself and don't deny your Creator's intended purpose for your life by set-tling for a lifetime of disrespect. In Christ's power, stand up and stop allowing your husband's abusive behavior to destroy your emotional and spiritual health as well as his own.

Trash Talk

How's it going with Ernie this week?" Rose asked Janice. "About the same," Janice answered. "He still hasn't put the window shutter back on the house. I asked him again Saturday for the hundredth time. I swear, that man never does anything around here without me constantly keeping on him. Being married to him is like having another kid!"

"So nothing's new then," Rose laughed.

With that short exchange, Rose and Janice moved on to another subject. These two friends commonly have conversations like that about Ernie, especially if something has recently happened that has caused Janice to become angry. Sometimes it's just a passing remark about him. At other times it's a full-blown rant about his shortcomings as a husband or a dad. Janice has similar conversations with others—even her weekly women's Bible study group.

Thus far in this book, we have primarily focused on husbands who (according to their wives) have misbehaved. In this chapter, we will focus more on how wives can unknowingly make matters worse.

Janice is actually a good woman. Most would even call her a godly woman. She's actively involved in ministry outreach through her local church. She volunteers her time to serve meals at a homeless shelter every week. She even has a devotional time with her Bible on her lap every morning. She's sincere and honestly wants to be a dedicated follower of Jesus Christ. But she is making a serious mistake that sometimes leads to disaster.

Janice and Ernie have been married 16 years. Ernie works hard delivering packages for FedEx. Janice is a homemaker who stays busy with her two adolescent children and her ministry outreach involvement. The two of them love each other, but over the past few years, their relationship has seemed to become increasingly stale.

Until Ernie started a new job at FedEx six years ago, the family took a vacation every year. Even if they only took the children on an overnight trip to a theme park a few hundred miles away, they always did something. Ernie and Janice also tried to get away for a weekend alone a few times a year. Grandparents would keep the children, and Ernie and Janice would enjoy themselves for a few days without the responsibility of the kids.

After Ernie began the new job, the trips became less frequent. His earnings had increased, but he often said he was too tired to do anything on the weekends. The children were now involved in soccer and dance classes as well as other activities. Janice was usually the one to shuttle them from one activity to the next. For a while, she wasn't bothered by Ernie being too tired to go anywhere or do anything, because she was tired too.

Over the past few years though, something began to change in their marriage. Nothing serious, but it was affecting the way they related to each other. They seldom argued, but Janice found herself feeling resentment toward Ernie. First he didn't want to do anything fun with her and the children, but now he didn't want to do much of anything at all. Life had become monotonous and predictable day after day, week after week, month after month. That gnawed at Janice.

Ernie didn't know she felt this way, but he did notice that she was often impatient with him about little things. He'd normally just let it go when she made a critical comment about his not having "moved that junk out of the garage," not having time to take their son to soccer practice, or not putting a shutter back on the window after the house was painted.

He was doing okay, but resentment was building in Janice with every new incident. None of the things were monumental. At times, she tried to understand why these incidental things triggered what she knew was a disproportionate level of irritation in her. None of them was a major problem, but the collective weight of Ernie's neglect about matters of house and home began to increase for Janice.

She had asked herself if she was wrong to feel the way she did, and she even prayed about it. She concluded that nothing was wrong with her believing that Ernie needed to fulfill certain responsibilities around the house and with the children. After all, she couldn't do it all alone. With two children and all the duties Ernie and she both had, two adults were necessary to keep things running smoothly.

Was Janice right in her assessment? Of course she was. Nobody could reasonably argue that Ernie shouldn't help with the children and household needs. He was misbehaving through his neglect.

Situations like the one Janice and Ernie experienced don't happen overnight. They occur little by little as bad behavior becomes worse until it finally comes to a tipping point in the spouse's mind. Ernie's lack of involvement progressed so gradually that Janice wasn't sure how to say exactly when it had started. All she knew for sure was that she didn't like it.

She first began to express her disapproval about Ernie's behavior to her close friend Rose a couple of years earlier. It began with her describing something Ernie had neglected to do and her response to it as if it there wasn't much to it. She talked about the situation in a casual and lighthearted way and often ended with a clever or humorous line about men in general.

As time passed, Janice began to speak more often about Ernie's shortcomings. The discussions began to include less humor and more frustration and displeasure about how Ernie was behaving. Rose's sympathetic reactions only validated Janice's complaints.

Gradually, Janice began to complain about Ernie to other friends too. Their responses varied. One would chime in about how her husband was the same as Ernie. Another would chide Janice for letting Ernie get away with that. Other friends would express sympathy and concern for Janice, telling her they would pray with her about the situation.

Janice didn't notice the way her habit of complaining to others about Ernie was affecting her marriage. Constantly verbalizing her discontent with her husband was counterproductive in several ways. She did notice that after she had criticized Ernie to somebody else, she felt negative emotions toward him when he came home from work.

As her friends affirmed her right to be upset with Ernie, she felt his offense against her and their home becoming bigger and harder to handle emotionally. She thought the situation needed to be resolved, and she was right about that. But the way she tried to find resolution just made matters worse.

One week, when her Bible study leader asked the ladies if there were things they wanted others to pray about, Janice mentioned her frustrations with Ernie. She described three times he had failed at home, just to make sure the other ladies understood the gravity of the problem and why it bothered her so much. As she had anticipated, they all were sympathetic about her situation.

What's Missing in This Picture?

Do you see anything wrong with the situation I've described with Janice and Ernie other than his bad behavior? I hope you can immediately see it because Ernie isn't the only one who is misbehaving. Janice is acting out too.

Have you noticed that I haven't mentioned whether Janice has sat down with Ernie and had a serious conversation with him about his misbehavior? She has taken verbal jabs at him. She has acted agitated toward him. She has let him know in nonverbal ways that his behavior is a problem, but she has not had a serious heart-to-heart talk with him about it. She probably thinks he should know there's a problem without having to be told. Regardless of whether she's right about that, the fact is, he doesn't know, and she hasn't told him in a way that he has understood.

Instead, she has gone to others and poured out her heart to them. There's one big problem with that approach—they can't change Ernie! The person Janice needs to talk with about her frustrations is the one person she hasn't seriously talked to about it.

Maybe your situation is similar to Janice's. Your husband is behaving irresponsibly in some way. His behavior might be completely different from Ernie's. It may not have anything to do with handling household responsibilities or helping with the children. It could be the way he talks to you, his irresponsibility with handling money, how much time he spends away from home with his hobby, or countless other misbehaviors. Ernie's misbehavior isn't the point.

I want you to zero in on the way Janice reacts to Ernie's bad behavior. She feels wounded by him and vindicated by her friends when she complains. That's a bad combination to perpetuate.

He Really Might Not Know

Many studies reveal that men are generally less relationally intuitive than women. Wives often sense that something is not right before their husbands even have a clue. Whether you believe a man should know when something's not right without being told is irrelevant. If he doesn't know, he doesn't know.

I've seen many wives raise the issue of divorce to their husbands only to discover that the guys are flabbergasted that anything at all has been wrong in their marriage. Everything was fine to them. You can argue all you want why this ought not be the case, but it is what it is, and chances are that unless your husband is a rare exception, he isn't as attuned to the things that frustrate you as you might wish he were.

If you are frustrated with any aspect of your husband's behavior, here is the key to the guidance I hope you find in this chapter: Talk *to* him and not *about* him. I do not mean to imply that you should never share your heart and hurt with a close friend. A good friend can indeed be a source of encouragement, but remember that if discussing your problem with your friend moves you further away from healing instead of toward it, you may need to rethink talking about it together. A true friend will certainly be sympathetic and will validate your feelings but will never nurture your sense of woundedness. Godly advice is always redemptive. It builds up and gives hope. It does not commiserate with the problem and join in with placing blame.

So talking to a true friend is fine, but talking negatively about your husband to many people isn't okay. People like Janice are often seeking to have a need met by others that their husbands are not meeting. They usually don't even realize they're doing anything wrong, but their actions can erode all hope for a better marriage.

The Emotional Power of Words

Have you noticed that when you discuss heart issues, you evoke an emotional response? When you tell your parent, your child, or your mate how much you love him or her, a corresponding feeling is aroused by just speaking those words. Words evoke feelings.

The same can be said about speaking negative things. When you criticize your husband to another person, you heighten your emotions. You actually solidify what you are feeling, and you fuel those emotions. That's one reason why repeatedly criticizing your husband to others can be destructive. If you add the validation you receive when others tell you you're right, you'll find that an internal prosecuting attorney will rise up inside your thoughts and emotions. He will not only prosecute but also judge and sometimes even sentence your husband for his behavior.

I hope you see the danger in speaking badly of your husband to other people. It's a bad habit that will lead to no good outcome. If there's a problem, talk with him about it. Notice I didn't say talk *to* him. To talk *with* your husband is to discuss the issue in a way that leaves both of you feeling as if you have been heard.

Aim for Understanding

Speak plainly but calmly to your husband about the problem as you understand it. Janice wouldn't need to unload 16 years of grievances on Ernie in a single conversation. She would simply need to summarize whatever she is unhappy about and then give just a few examples of Ernie's behavior as illustrations.

Speak matter-of-factly about your concerns. Don't allow your tone or volume to make your husband feel as if you're attacking him. You might be justified in doing that, but the goal of the conversation is to accomplish good, and that would do no good. Instead, it would likely trigger a defense mechanism in him. Speak directly but calmly about your complaint.

Then ask him to tell you, in his own words, what he has heard you say. If he becomes defensive, remind him that you're simply asking him to tell you what he heard so that you'll know whether you've been clear. If he simply parrots what you've said, ask him to tell you in his own words so you can know he understands.

Don't move past this step until you are satisfied that he has understood you. If you skip past this important part of communication, the conversation will degenerate into a dispute. You'll just be trying to make him acknowledge guilt that he cannot and will not see. Take your time and don't allow him to hijack the conversation and take the lead so that the discussion deteriorates. Stay focused on your concern until he demonstrates that he has heard and understood it. Your goal at this point is not to come to an agreement, but to be understood.

How the conversation moves forward from this point will depend on your husband's response. Once you know he has understood your concern, you can ask him if he would like to work together to resolve the matter. As you discuss resolution together, take the time to respond to what he has said just as you've asked him to do with your words. Rephrase what you've heard him say to you so he will know you are listening and understanding him.

The goal in this type of discussion is primarily to promote understanding. Misunderstanding causes more friction between married couples than does most anything else. Work together toward understanding before attempting to move toward finding agreement. You'll discover that when you understand each other, agreement will come much more readily.

Ernie loves Janice, but until Janice sits down and has this sort of conversation with him, things are unlikely to get any better. She may feel moments of justification about her frustrations with Ernie by talking about him to her friends, but her underlying resentment will only continue to grow over time. That's dangerous because unresolved resentment is often the seed to ultimate disaster in a marriage. Sometimes it leads to divorce. Sometimes it leads to a situation that can be as painful as divorce—a dead marriage in which a couple just coexists together without passion for their relationship.

Be careful not to mishandle this kind of communication. If you do, you could short-circuit your chance of resolving negative issues in your marriage. Your husband may indeed be misbehaving, but talking to others about him instead of talking with him about the problem will only make matters worse.

Greener Grass

*I*t all started so innocently. Kimberly would never have said she and Gordon had marriage problems. Her husband was a good man. He just wasn't very demonstrative about much of anything. The most enthusiasm she ever saw him express was when he was watching football on television.

Still, all in all, he wasn't a bad guy. He was a good provider. She and Gordon both had good jobs. She usually worked between 20 and 25 hours a week in the office at a car dealership. Gordon put in more than 40 hours on his job because he often worked Saturdays to earn overtime income. When he wasn't at work, he spent most evenings tinkering on an old Studebaker he had bought a few years ago and had been restoring ever since. Some of Kimberly's friends said their husbands were seldom home because they were always hunting, fishing, or playing golf. Gordon wasn't like that. He was home most of the time. He was a good man.

Though he seldom showed affection, Gordon was always respectful toward Kimberly. He never criticized her in front of people the way she had seen a few of her friends' husbands do. In fact, he seldom had anything negative to say at home either. He just went about his day and allowed Kimberly to do the same.

There were things that used to bother her, but not now. If she didn't remind him that their wedding anniversary was coming up, he wouldn't remember it. That had caused big arguments early in their marriage, but Kimberly had solved that by reminding him every year. It was no big deal. Once she started doing that, he had never missed buying her something for their special day. She didn't know whether he would remember if she didn't remind him, but that was okay. She didn't mind mentioning it every year. Overall, everything was good. It wasn't a bad situation—not at all.

Jeff was a salesman at the dealership where Kimberly worked. Everybody liked him. He was an extrovert with a good sense of humor. He was a natural focal point and catalyst for the playful banter that went on all day among his coworkers. He was quick with clever quips and could see humor in almost any situation.

Jeff was also a considerate man. Kimberly had seen him go above and beyond to help people, like the time he drove a fair distance out of his way to pick up a coworker who needed a ride for a few days while his own car was in the shop for repairs. Jeff was that kind of man. He was always doing something for somebody. Kimberly had noticed this on numerous occasions.

One Monday afternoon, Kimberly and six others went to lunch together. Normally, only two or three at a time would leave for lunch, but this had been an especially slow day. Jeff was in the group too.

As the host showed the group to their table, Kimberly watched where Jeff sat and went around the table to sit beside him. The lunch was enjoyable, and as usual, Jeff kept the conversation lively and laughter hearty. Kimberly really enjoyed the time.

When they all went to the cashier to pay for their meals, Kimberly noticed a bowl of Peppermint Patties on the counter for the guests. She took one and slid the bowl toward Jeff. "Want one?" she asked.

"No thanks, I don't like them," Jeff answered.

"What? I love them! Okay, now you've lost my respect," Kimberly joked.

"I do hate that," Jeff said, smiling. "But they're too sweet for me. I guess I'm sweet enough already."

"And I'm not?" Kimberly playfully asked.

"I didn't say that." Jeff smiled.

No harm had been done. It was simply innocent banter between two coworkers.

As the weeks passed, Kimberly began enjoying Jeff's presence at work more and more. Nothing was said or done that anybody could consider wrong. Kimberly knew she liked Jeff, but didn't everybody?

One day when Jeff and another salesman came back from lunch, he walked over to her desk. "I brought you something," he said, pulling a handful of Peppermint Patties out of his pocket and laying them on her desk.

"Thanks!" Kimberly said. "What's this about?"

"Ron and I ate at Frescos again today, and when I saw these, I thought of you," Jeff said.

It was a small thing, an insignificant thing, nothing at all, but Kimberly liked it. She liked it a lot. Jeff had remembered she liked the treats and had brought her some.

As time passed, Kimberly reached the point where she couldn't deny it anymore. There were vibes between Jeff and her. Since the day he had said, "You look really nice today," she had put forth extra effort to be sure she dressed her best for work. She found herself hoping off and on through the day that Jeff would come off the sales floor into the office so they could talk. And he did—more and more as the weeks passed. She looked forward to these moments every day.

For the longest time, neither of them said anything that kept them from rationalizing their misbehavior. The truth was, though, they both knew they were crossing lines that friends shouldn't cross if either is married. The compliments, the prolonged eye contact, and the occasional touch on the shoulder or arm were beginning to take on a life of their own.

Jeff's attention toward Kimberly obviously increased. One morning when they coincidentally drove into the parking lot at work at the same time and were approaching the door into the building together, Jeff looked her up and down and simply said, "Wow." Kimberly slapped his arm and said, "Behave!" but they both knew she liked it. Vibes were evolving into chemistry.

Now, let's leave this discussion of Kimberly and Gordon and Jeff right there. Here are a few questions to consider. What do you think is going to happen? Has Kimberly done anything wrong yet? Has Jeff? Does Gordon fit into what is going on at work between Kimberly and Jeff?

We're All Needy People

This kind of situation happens every day in the workplace with more people than you might imagine. Don't think for a moment that believers in Christ are exempt from this kind of subtle situation or that it doesn't lead to big trouble. If you think you're exempt, you're in the dangerous place of not knowing the potential we all have for wrongdoing.

Kimberly isn't a bad person. As my description of her interaction with Jeff ends, she has no intention of committing adultery with Jeff. None. However, that doesn't mean it won't end up happening. It simply hasn't entered her mind...yet.

We are all born with three basic needs in life: to be loved, to be accepted, and to be appreciated. We all want those things. Our Creator has left that three-pronged receptacle in us so He can be the One to meet those needs. It's what has been called a God-shaped vacuum. Those fundamental needs reside in every human being.

In a healthy marriage, God intends to meet those three needs primarily through our mate. Our spouse isn't the one who meets the needs, but God satisfies those needs *through* our mate. That's true for both husbands and wives.

If I were writing to husbands, at this point I would discuss how a husband is to meet these core needs in his wife. But your husband isn't reading this book, so I'll address your vulnerability when you don't allow God to be the One who meets your needs for love, acceptance, and appreciation.

Unless a wife has these three needs met through her relationship to God, she is at risk of trying to gain love, acceptance, and appreciation from a wrong source. Can you see this happening with Kimberly? She's not out there looking for another man, but she does want her three basic needs to be met, and for the moment, she *feels* as if Jeff is meeting those needs.

Emotional Adultery

I mentioned that Kimberly has no intention of committing adultery. However, she doesn't realize that the vibes that have already turned into chemistry will lead to sexual tension if she doesn't stop now. It won't be because her appetite for a sexual relationship with Jeff will suddenly surge. It will happen because the gratification she feels from Jeff's growing attention and gushing approval will stir up emotions and desires that become blurry and blended. It won't be about the sex for her. It will be about the gratification of having a man adore and affirm her the way Jeff does.

I've seen this scenario many times, and you've probably seen it too. Infidelity doesn't generally happen with wives because they are attracted to a sexual relationship. It happens because they want to feel the fire of being passionately loved, accepted, and appreciated.

Identifying how frequently adultery occurs in society is a difficult challenge. Pollsters agree that people are often hesitant to be honest about the topic. Psychologist and author Dr. Bonnie Eaker Weil suggests that "more than 50 percent of all married women, at some point, cheat on their mates."* That number seems high to many of us. Some polls report lower numbers, but others report as high as 65 percent. The point is, adultery is a pervasive societal problem.

When a wife walks in grace, she isn't naive about the potential for

---

* "Who's Likely to Cheat?" abcnews.go.com/2020/story?id=124040&page=1#.UESorFS_vlo.

developing an unhealthy relationship with other men. We'll never know how many wives find themselves in relationships like the one between Kimberly and Jeff. How would you describe their relationship? Any wise person would say it is unhealthy at best. Would you go so far as to call it emotional adultery?

Emotional adultery involves a heart connection beyond friendship that joins a married person to another in an intimate way without sexual involvement. It is charged with sexual energy, romantic feelings, or feelings of intimacy that go further than what should exist in a healthy friendship. It always causes a "rush" and a desire to see the other person as much as possible. An unwise woman might argue, "We've done nothing wrong." But wisdom recognizes that this kind of connection to a man other than one's husband is dangerous and must be abandoned immediately.

As I write this chapter, I am confident that you would never want to fall into an adulterous relationship. You wouldn't be reading a book that centers on God's grace if your head and heart were in that place. However, emotional adultery is insidious. Even sincere women of integrity can find themselves caught up in it without having had any plans to do anything wrong. "It just happened," they often explain, but the reality is that these things don't just happen. Rather, people close their eyes to what is going on along the way.

Warning Signs

A number of warning signs can alert you that an inappropriate relationship is developing. If you see any of these indicators in one of your relationships, take notice. The situation may seem innocuous now, but it can lead to a place you don't want to go.

- Do you often hope you will see someone because of the way he makes you feel?

- Do you confide with a male friend about personal matters of the heart more than you do with your own husband?

- Does thinking about him affect the way you dress, wear your hair, or decide on perfume, nail polish, or anything else related to your appearance?

- Would you be uncomfortable telling your husband every detail about your relationship with this person, including how you feel and think when you're with him?

Healthy relationships can exist between married people of the opposite sex, but don't be naive or in denial about a potentially dangerous relationship with another man. If you are intentionally avoiding mentioning the man to your husband, that is a warning sign. If you are mentally comparing your husband to this man, that is a warning sign.

When unhealthy relationships begin to develop, wives commonly begin to compare in this way. Kimberly surely would have noted that Gordon had to be reminded of their wedding anniversary every year but that Jeff remembered something as incidental as her fondness for Peppermint Patties. Kimberly would easily begin to see many of Gordon's shortcomings in contrast to Jeff's strengths. The comparison would likely cause a strain in her relationship to Gordon. They would likely begin arguing more as Kimberly distanced herself emotionally from Gordon and became more and more attracted to Jeff.

The Physiology of Attraction

I mentioned earlier in the chapter that the chemistry between Kimberly and Jeff would turn to sexual tension if she didn't stop the relationship immediately. The importance of this can't be overstated. Kimberly doesn't realize that the further this goes, the more dangerous it becomes, and not just from an emotional standpoint. Before long, her actual physiology will pull her deeper into her destructive behavior.

Sexual attention caused by physical attraction can actually increase dopamine, a hormone that produces feelings of pleasure, as well as norepinephrine, which is similar to adrenaline and increases excitement. So Kimberly's mind, her emotions, and even her physical body are affected by her inappropriate relationship with Jeff. What began so innocently has now morphed into an ugly trap that has snared her hook, line, and sinker. Sadly, the time may come when she will honestly say, "I didn't mean for it to happen."

Kimberly will be telling the truth, but had she known the warning signs, she could have recognized what was going on and stopped it before things gained momentum.

Was Kimberly's husband, Gordon, complicit in this whole matter? Of course, but he's not reading this book. You are, and I hope that even if your husband fails you in certain areas, you will keep your eyes wide open and observe the warning signs in situations that could lead to a bad place. The grass may look greener, but the reality is that this kind of wrong decision inevitably scorches our lives.

Rearing Children

"Boys will be boys, Nicole!"

"Well, boys need to learn to behave, Art!" Nicole countered as her irritation obviously increased.

For the past half hour, the two had been discussing their son, Michael, who had that day brought home his third demerit report for misbehaving in class during the past month. This time the teacher had jotted a note across the bottom to Nicole and Art. "Could you call me at your convenience to set up a meeting to discuss Michael's behavior in class?"

When Nicole saw the note, she became angry. At least that's how she reacted to Michael when she told him to put down his video game controller and go to his bedroom. She actually felt completely frustrated because she didn't know what to do. She left Michael in his room for an hour and a half until Art came home from work. Now she and he were not seeing eye to eye about the importance of this matter.

Art and Nicole are in their midthirties with two children—Michael, who is twelve, and Emily, who is eight. Since Michael started attending a new school this year, his behavior at school and at home has worsened. Nicole works mornings as the secretary at the small church the family attends. She is always home when the bus delivers the children from school, so she has time with them every day before Art comes home from work.

Nicole's frustration with Michael is over things that are typical of boys his age. He wants to spend all his time playing video games and has to be reminded that he must do his homework first. He complains at times about not being allowed to do what other kids get to do. Now and then he will speak to Nicole in a disrespectful way, frequently asking "Why not?" in a tone that sounds more like an accusation than a question. None of the things Michael does are serious, but Nicole is concerned they could be ominous signs of things to come. His attitude troubles her, and she wants to nip it in the bud before his behavior becomes worse.

Michael tends to keep it all in line, for the most part, when Art is home. He will occasionally flare up, but usually after one stern correction from Art, the matter is dropped. It seldom works that way with Nicole and Michael. He has learned just how far he can push her, and he typically takes it to the limit when he is denied his way.

Nicole has tried to talk with Art about her frustration with Michael's misbehavior, but he never seems to take it very seriously. When the third report came from school and the teacher requested to meet with Art and Nicole, Nicole's frustration escalated higher than ever before. How can the matter be resolved if they go to meet with the teacher and Art doesn't take the problem seriously?

You're Not Alone

This kind of issue often happens among parents. If you feel helpless to know whether you are doing your part to help your children grow up into mature and responsible adults, you're not alone. All parents feel that way at times.

Nicole and Art often don't agree on the best approach to take when disciplining the children, but that's just one of the areas couples grapple with as they attempt to be good parents. When the children are small, parenting is labor intensive, to put it mildly. Almost every detail of children's lives has to be negotiated and carried out by moms and dads who need to work in sync to accomplish what's best for the children.

As children reach adolescence, a whole new set of variables have to be considered. Is the child old enough for this? Should that be allowed? Would this entertainment be age appropriate? The questions only increase between childhood and the adolescent years.

Before they know it, parents are facing the teen years, and perhaps the most difficult time in parenting is upon them. How much freedom is a teen to be given? How far should the teen be allowed to adapt to the popular styles in music, dress, pastimes, and the like? Issues seemed to be simple puzzles when the children were small, but they evolve into a complicated maze of uncertainty during the teen years.

One big reason parenting is so challenging is that it's not an exact science. There is no perfect formula that guarantees that your child will turn out exactly the way you hope. People like Nicole and Art certainly want to rear their children in a biblical manner, but identifying precisely what that means and how to effectively apply it in real life isn't as clear-cut as they might wish.

As a wife who walks in grace, you undoubtedly want to do the best job you can in rearing your children. You want them to become adults who possess faith and integrity, people who will be well equipped to successfully navigate whatever situations they may encounter in life. You realize that the way you parent your children now will have lasting results later. For that reason you want to do this well.

What can you do as a wife and mother that will maximize your children's potential to become the people you want them to be?

As I've stated, there is no exact formula for rearing children. But there are some biblical approaches to child rearing that would serve people like Nicole and Art well. These may be helpful as you assess your own approach to parenting.

Maintain Unified Guidance

This is one of the most important parenting principles: You and your husband must act as one when dealing with your children. Art and Nicole aren't on the same page about child rearing, and as a result, they are addressing Michael's behavior inconsistently as well as increasing tension in their own relationship. Children must see their parents as a unified presence.

Consider your heavenly Father. Can you imagine Him and Jesus Christ taking different approaches toward you? What if one took one approach toward you and the other had a completely different approach? Jesus told His disciples, "I and the Father are one" (John 10:30). Another time, He said, "He who has seen me has seen the Father" (John 14:9). The Father, Son, and Spirit are all in union and share the same mind and heart toward His children.

One day when Art came home from work, Michael was playing a video game, and Nicole was upstairs. "Have you done your homework?" Art asked.

"I'm about to do it," Michael answered.

"Go do it," Art responded.

"Can't I just finish this game? It'll only take five more minutes," Michael said.

"Okay, but you finish *that* game only, then get on your homework."

How might Art's handling of this particular situation affect Michael? At that moment, Art completely failed to demonstrate unity with Nicole in teaching Michael how to behave. To the contrary, he undermined the stability and structure that had supposedly been set in place when Michael had first been told that homework comes before play.

Sometimes the parents aren't consistent at all. Imagine if Nicole had come downstairs and found Michael playing the video game. What if she had been really tired that day and was too frustrated to confront Michael and insist that he put the game down and do his homework? How would that have affected Michael's obedience over the long haul?

One frustrated young mother once told me during counseling, "Sometimes I'm just too tired to fight those battles." In other words, "It's easier just to give in than to be bothered with a parenting moment that requires more energy than I want to give at the time." That may be true, and it may indeed make things easier in that moment, but at what cost?

Are you and your husband consistently unified in your approach to parenting? Does your child fully know that when it comes to discipline and obedience, if he has heard Mom, he has heard Dad? If you truthfully examine your joint parenting effort and don't readily see a unified guidance with your children, discuss this issue with your husband and determine together how to resolve this matter.

Focus on Identity

Teaching children to behave is often the most time-consuming expenditure of energy in parenting. Given your desire to invest in your children's lives and the monumental importance of the task, perhaps the wisest thing you can ask yourself is, "What is the most important thing I can impart to my child?"

Think about that question for a moment. What is the most important thing you can impart to your child during these years? How can you lay the best foundation for his whole life? What do you want your children to take with them, guiding and influencing them all throughout their lives?

Too often, parents focus on appropriate behavior but neglect a matter of much greater importance. The right kind of behavior certainly is important, not only during childhood but also throughout life. But the question is, what will be the impetus for your children's good behavior once your immediate supervision is no longer available?

The answer to that question has to do with your child's identity. Knowing the bounds of right behavior is important, but when a person has built a secure self-awareness of an honorable identity, that will become the guiding light throughout life. Nobody will consistently behave in a way that contradicts her perception of who she really is. In other words, for the most part, people will act according to who they think they are.

For that reason, if your children are to walk in grace, it is essential that they learn who they are. They must know their identity in Jesus Christ. The nature of our identity is rooted in the spirit level of our being. A person's body doesn't define her. Somebody's soul (his mind, emotions, and will) doesn't give him his personhood. Our authentic selves are defined in our spirits. We all are spirit beings who live in bodies and possess souls.

Your Child's True Identity

It is important to focus on this—instilling in our children a secure sense that above all, they are created to experience and express God's love. Your child is a spirit being whom the God of the universe deeply loves! The fact that God loves each of us gives us our value. Immediately after God created Adam and Eve, He blessed them (Genesis 5:2). Our existence as human beings originates in God's love. His sustaining love enables us to be who we were created to be.

The most important thing you can teach your children, the most important thing they can know, is that God unconditionally loves them. The desire to be accepted and appreciated is the desire to feel loved. Children need to know that the love of God is secure and constant, independent of anything they may or may not do, both now and throughout their lives. Much misbehavior in life is a misguided attempt to feel loved, appreciated, and accepted. Lay the proper foundation in your child's life early on, and he will be equipped to avoid many potential pitfalls later in life.

Obviously, parents must deal with behavior in their children's lives. One key is the way we choose to handle behavior. Never call your child a bad boy. Instead, teach him that God has created him to be a good boy and that as a good boy, he must learn not to do bad things. Do you see the difference? One approach establishes or reinforces a negative and false identity. The other affirms a good and biblical identity while not ignoring bad behavior.

The goal is not to give your child a good self-image, but to help her develop a self-image prescribed by our Creator. We are who God says we are. As you lay the foundation for your children's future, be diligent to teach them who God says they are. Let that be the starting place as you teach them why certain behaviors are acceptable and others are unacceptable.

If you don't feel equipped to teach your children the biblical truth about who they are in Christ, you may find it helpful to first study that subject. Unless we know our identity in Him and are able to teach that to our children, our parenting default will be to establish good behavior. To put that first is to place things in reverse order. A person may know what the right behavior is and still consistently choose wrong, but when the truth about his God-given identity becomes a conscious part of the fiber of his being, he will be infinitely better equipped to make right choices over wrong ones.

Like Art and Nicole, you and your husband want to teach your child to make responsible and healthy choices. That outcome doesn't happen automatically. There are no guarantees in life concerning what your children will or won't do when they are old enough to make independent decisions, but you have fulfilled your role when, as a unified team, you and your husband have taught them who they are in Jesus Christ and who He is in them.

Doing the right thing in life comes most naturally when a person has a biblical concept of being the right person. Help your child understand how to live in a way that is compatible with her authentic self, and she will become the person her Creator has designed her to be. That, in the end, is what parenting is all about.

Festering Wounds

*I*t had happened three years earlier when Dylan was spending so much time out of state handling a big account that required a lot of hands-on involvement. In fact, it was the company's largest account, and Dylan was actually complimented by the fact that he was the one who was asked to go.

For eight months, he spent two weeks out of every month in Houston, helping the Zyrex Group train their employees to use a new software package they had recently installed. He walked them through the frequent IT bumps that came whenever a company made such a big change. He stayed in an extended-stay suite at the same hotel every time. His wife, Kayla, wasn't crazy about him being gone so much, but they both understood this kind of commitment could bring the big promotion they had been hoping would come.

About four months into this routine, Kayla began to notice something different in Dylan's demeanor when he was at home. She couldn't identify exactly what it was, but he didn't seem himself. She asked him several times if he was okay, and he always assured her he was. She believed him.

Three more months passed. While Dylan was taking a shower, Kayla was in the living room watching the evening news on TV.

She was waiting for their son, Devin, to text or call to let her know that his ball practice was over and that she could come get him. She heard the "ding" on Dylan's cell phone that indicated he had received a text message.

Thinking it might be Devin, she picked up Dylan's phone to check. The message simply asked, "Are you at home?" Scrolling up and looking at the previous text, Kayla made a horrible discovery that would change her life. The text was from another woman. As she read the exchange between them, Kayla had no doubt. Dylan had been having an affair.

I met Kayla three years later. She and Dylan were still married, but their relationship changed the day she had read the text, and they still hadn't recovered. Kayla questioned if things could ever be normal again. As we talked together, Kayla wondered how Dylan had come to do "such a horrible thing."

"It's not like we didn't have a good marriage," she said. "Or so I thought. I've always been attentive and affectionate to him. He seemed happy too, but if he was happy and really loved me, why would he do such a horrible thing to me?"

The situation became clear to me over a period of several sessions as Kayla explained the details. She and Dylan hadn't experienced any serious problems in their marriage until he made the choice to become involved with a woman in Houston. Kayla verified through cell phone bills that the affair had begun three months before she caught Dylan. It was around the time she had begun to notice that he wasn't acting like himself when he came home from Houston.

On the day that she caught and confronted Dylan, she took Devin and spent the next week with her parents, who lived in the same town. Dylan called her cell phone repeatedly all week, but she wouldn't take his call. When he called her parents' house, her mother told him, "Kayla needs some time to think."

At first, Kayla intended to divorce Dylan. After what he had done, she could see no way their marriage could ever be restored. By

the end of the week, she was having second thoughts about her decision. She thought about the changes divorce would bring to Devin's
life. She thought about the idea of being single again. She contem-
plated many matters during that week, but the biggest thing she
couldn't shake was that she loved Dylan. Although she was deeply
hurt and passionately angry, she still loved him.

After a week, Kayla and Devin went back home again. She slept
in the guest bedroom. Right away, Dylan began to try to make
things right with her. It was obvious he didn't want a divorce.

"He said it meant nothing," she told me one day. "They all say
that! It may have meant nothing to *him*, but his stupidity destroyed
us!"

After Kayla had poured out her anger, I quietly asked, "So what
do you want to do?"

"I want to go back in time and make this not happen!"

"I wish that could be done too," I answered, "but you are where
you are, and now you have to decide what you're going to do. Three
years have passed, and you two haven't been able to move beyond
what he did. Do you still love him?"

"Yes," she quietly replied.

"Do you believe he really loves you?" I asked.

"Oh, I have no doubt about that," Kayla answered. "He's grov-
eled and begged for my forgiveness for three years. He tries to do
anything I want and would do anything to get me past this."

"Do you want to get past it?" I asked her.

"Of course I do. This hasn't just affected our relationship. I've
been turning into somebody I don't like since all this happened."

"Have you forgiven him?" I asked.

"Well, if staying with him these past three years hasn't shown him
I've forgiven him, I don't know what would. Anybody else would
have left, and I've often thought I should have," Kayla answered.

Kayla's response to my question revealed that she probably didn't
understand much about forgiveness. She hadn't left Dylan, and she

believed that proved she had forgiven him. She couldn't have been more wrong.

Understanding Forgiveness

Forgiveness is one of the most misunderstood aspects of the process of healing after someone has hurt us. The act of forgiving another person clears the way for divine healing. No wonder the enemy of our souls doesn't want us to correctly understand what it means to forgive another person.

A number of misunderstandings about forgiveness often keeps wounded people from truly extending forgiveness to those who have hurt them. Without moving beyond these misunderstandings and discovering the true meaning of forgiveness, a person like Kayla will never be completely free from the effect of the offense committed against her.

It has often been said that time heals all wounds. Nothing could be further from the truth. Unless we extend forgiveness, the wounds that others inflict on us can poison our thoughts, emotions, and actions for as long as we live. In fact, given enough time, withholding forgiveness from those who have hurt us can cripple us in many ways. To believe that time heals all wounds is a serious mistake. Time itself will prove that it won't.

Kayla believed that her choice to stay with Dylan despite what he had done was evidence of forgiveness. Her viewpoint is a common misunderstanding. The idea is that if we do our best to put an offense against us aside and act as if it didn't happen, things will get better. Kayla's comment that anybody else would have left Dylan shows her wrong thinking about what forgiveness means. She assumed that since she didn't leave, she had obviously forgiven him. But here she was three years later, souring more and more on the inside.

Don't make the same mistake. You may try to ignore your pain, but that does not indicate that you've forgiven the one who hurt you. That's not what forgiveness is, and to think otherwise will hold you indefinitely in a wounded place. The fact that you "let it go" and don't seek revenge or dole out punishment in no way means you have extended forgiveness toward an offender. You may think you can let it go, but it won't let *you* go until you forgive those who hurt you.

As I explained the meaning of forgiveness to her one day, Kayla brought up a common objection about forgiving the one who has hurt us. "I wish I could forgive him like that, but I can't. I can't help being angry, and to say that I forgive Dylan would be a lie. I don't feel like forgiving him, and I'd be a hypocrite to say I do."

This opinion may be the most frequently used reason for not forgiving another person. The idea is that if we still feel angry, we must not yet be able to honestly forgive. The problem with that viewpoint is that it wrongly assumes that forgiving somebody requires our emotions to line up with our decision to forgive. That faulty understanding can hold an offended person in an emotional prison for a long time.

What Is Forgiveness?

Forgiveness is the conscious choice to release a person from an offense that he has committed against us. It is a choice we make, not an emotion we feel. Feelings gradually heal after we have extended forgiveness to somebody. They don't heal instantly.

Hypocrisy refers to behavior that is contradictory to who we really are. The English word "hypocrite" came from the arts and refers to somebody who is acting on a stage, pretending to be somebody he isn't. Hypocrisy has nothing to do with actions that contradict your feelings. It has to do with acting in a way that contradicts who you really are.

Who are you? You are one who has Jesus Christ living inside you. He has given you an identity that exists in union with His indwelling life. Jesus Christ defines you. It is your nature to extend forgiveness because the One who establishes your true identity is a forgiving person. He is the core of your authentic self, so it is your nature to extend forgiveness too.

Kayla had already determined that she loved Dylan and had no intention of leaving him. But apart from forgiving him, what kind of life would they have together? She was being changed by the poisonous effect of not forgiving her husband. She needed to forgive Dylan for their sake, but she also needed to forgive him for her own sake.

In Isaiah 43:25, God provides important insight about the matter of forgiveness: "I, even I, am the one who wipes out your transgressions for My own sake, and I will not remember your sins." This verse reveals an interesting reason why God forgives. He said He forgives for His own sake.

It's important for you to release your husband from any wrong he has committed against you, not only for his sake but also for your own sake. Otherwise, the harm done to you will fester inside you and gradually change you in ways you don't want to be changed. You need to forgive for *you*.

The objection that the person who committed the offense doesn't deserve to be forgiven often comes up when this subject is discussed. "Do you mean I should just let him get away with it and act like it never happened?" One wife said to me, "I'm the one who has to pay the price while he goes on with no real consequences!"

This is where it becomes very apparent that forgiveness is an expression of grace. Of course the one who hurt you doesn't deserve forgiveness. Grace causes us to release a person from the wrong he has done even though he doesn't merit that forgiveness. Nobody ever deserves forgiveness. To forgive is to put away the wrongdoing and stop holding it against the one who did it despite the fact that he doesn't deserve such kindness.

Forgiving doesn't mean we act as if something never happened. To the contrary, we fully embrace what has happened. We acknowledge the offense. We own it and grieve it. Then we dis-charge the debt we believe the other person owes us. We willfully release the person from owing us anything.

When God says He will no longer remember our sins, the Bible doesn't mean that He imposes amnesia on Himself. He doesn't for-get. God knows everything, and that doesn't change. The idea that He doesn't remember has a fuller meaning than divine forgetfulness.

Imagine somebody accidentally cutting off her finger in an acci-dent. Most people would know they should wrap the severed fin-ger in ice and rush both the finger and the victim to the hospital. Upon arrival, the patient would probably be rushed into the oper-ating room, where a surgeon would attempt to re-member the fin-ger to the hand.

So to re-member is to attach the member back to where it came from. When the Bible says God won't remember our sins, it means that He will never attach them to us again. They will never be re-membered. He has chosen to detach them from us and never to con-nect us to them again.

That's what it means to forgive another person. Will you forget what he has done? No, but if you choose to release him from the offense and refuse to ever attach that deed to him again, you have forgiven. Your choice to forgive is the result of your volition, not your emotion.

To walk in grace is to forgive others. There is probably no place in your life where forgiveness is more important than in your mar-riage. This subject is worthy of your time and prayerful consider-ation if you need to forgive. Having counseled people for 40 years, I have seen that in many instances where a couple can't seem to get along without constant bickering, there are underlying issues of unforgiveness.

If you have stuffed away the hurts your husband has commit-ted against you, and you are assuming that if you ignore them long enough everything will be okay, you are making a serious mistake.

People who ignore cuts often end up with infections. Those infections can lead to gangrene and catastrophic endings. Don't allow that to happen in your marriage.

Ask the Spirit of Jesus, who lives inside you, to show you where you need to forgive. When He brings incidents to mind, don't rationalize them away. Forgive those who have hurt you, and you'll discover a cleansing, healing effect in your emotions, thoughts, and possibly even your body.

13

Religious Arguments

The age-old question has been debated since Old Testament times. Carrie knew better than to allow herself to be drawn in to the debate, but being an extroverted, verbal processor, she couldn't resist the urge. Now she felt as if Drew had once again demonstrated to his own satisfaction why her faith was without evidence or substance.

They had been watching TV when a commercial about the terrible plight of children in a third-world country had played. "Show your love to one of God's precious children by sponsoring a child right now," the announcer said.

"Seems like it's God who's not doing a very good job of showing love to His child," Drew quipped, glancing over toward Carrie. She saw his glance in her peripheral vision but quietly stared at the TV. "Using God to milk money for their pet project seems about as low as it gets," Drew continued, this time with derision in his voice.

"Using money to feed starving children isn't what I'd call 'milking money from people for a pet project,'" Carrie answered, obviously irritated.

"Well, what else would you call it?" Drew responded. "Besides, those children probably don't see more than pennies on the dollar."

Again, Carrie remained silent.

"If God is love, why does He even need organizations like that? If He really was love, He wouldn't allow children to suffer that way to begin with."

That was the burning fuse that started it all. For the next half hour Carrie found herself debating the ancient question of how God can be love and yet allow suffering in this world. The conversation quickly turned into an argument.

"This is how it always works," Carrie told me in my office. "He deliberately baits me, and if I react, he turns it into an argument. But if I don't say anything, he makes blatant statements about God or Christianity that aren't true. To stand by silently while he slams my faith doesn't seem like the right thing to do. But to answer him starts an argument that usually leaves me feeling angry and leaves him acting smug and pompous."

Surprisingly, Drew attends church with Carrie every week. When he is there, he is courteous to everybody. Nobody would imagine these arguments were frequently occurring at home. "It seems like he only goes to church with me to find things to criticize later," Carrie once told me.

Despite the fact that Carrie urged Drew to come to counseling with her, I never had the opportunity to meet him. I did learn that Drew's attitude toward spiritual matters hadn't always been this way. Things changed when they had been a part of a different local church, where a leader Drew respected had been discovered in an affair with a woman also in the church. He spoke with harsh contempt about the leader for too long in Carrie's opinion. "He wouldn't let it go," she said.

The leader left the church, but the whole incident planted a seed of cynicism in Drew that had sprouted and grown. He had little patience with anything at church that seemed inauthentic, and his reaction at home seemed disproportionate to the actual situation. Carrie tolerated his attitude about those things, but now that his snide remarks were often directed toward God Himself, she wasn't sure what to do.

The Best Thing to Say

Knowing how to respond to a mate who is often critical of the very thing that is most personal and dear to you can be challenging. Carrie felt that if she said nothing to counter Drew's slurs against God, she would compromise her faith. On the other hand, time had proven that she could not win those arguments regardless of what she said. The situation seemed hopeless.

Maybe you've found yourself in a similar place at times. What you're going to read in this chapter about responding to a husband who seems to enjoy provoking arguments over spiritual matters can help in any situation like this, not just at home. Perhaps this kind of situation exists in your relationship with your husband, but even if you're on the same page about spiritual matters, this chapter can still help. We all encounter people who like to argue. Recognition and application of a few simple truths about how to respond to people like Drew can bring real peace to your own emotions and can stabilize tense situations like the one I've described with this couple.

What is the best way to respond if your husband tries to provoke an argument about spiritual things? Don't. That's right. Often the best way to respond is by not responding. There are many reasons why certain people seem to enjoy arguing about spiritual issues, but there is never a good reason to engage with such provocation over these matters.

There is a huge difference between discussions and even healthy debates on one hand and arguments on the other. Healthy discussion and debate is a mutual search for truth, a verbal give-and-take as people work together to discover or clarify a particular truth. There can be real value in that kind of exchange. Healthy debate can be spirited and impassioned and still be a good thing if those involved are behaving with respect to each other and as long as the motivation is a sincere desire to grow in the knowledge of the truth.

Arguing about spiritual matters is another issue altogether. Arguments don't move toward the common goal of identifying and embracing truth. The goal of an argument is to establish oneself as a winner and the other person as a loser. Arguments aren't fueled by a desire for the truth but by the prideful desire to prove oneself to be right.

The Holy Spirit is gladly engaged in the passionate discourse of people who are wrestling to know truth. However, He absolutely will not be involved in an argument. Agape simply will not behave that way.

If your husband's comments provoke and agitate you, it is probably a good idea simply not to respond. That's true about comments regarding spiritual subjects, but it's also good advice regardless of the topic. Helpful discussions seldom begin from a starting place of agitated emotions. If the Holy Spirit can't guide the conversation, what's the point in going there? Nothing good can come from it.

Perhaps the better thing to do is to refuse to be drawn into the conversation. You can remain silent. You can change the subject. If you are cornered and feel that you must speak, you can simply answer, "I suspect you know that's not my opinion on the matter, but I'd rather not discuss it right now."

Refuse to be pulled into a conversation you don't want to have. The best way to keep from losing a tug-of-war is to simply drop the rope. Don't pick it up, or drop it when you see what it has become. You alone have the power to determine what you will and won't engage in verbally.

Paul wrote Timothy about what to teach people concerning this very subject: "Warn them before God against pious nitpicking, which chips away at the faith. It just wears everyone out" (2 Timothy 2:14 MSG).

If you've argued about spiritual things, you know firsthand that what Paul told Timothy is true. It's not just a waste of time and energy. It is spiritually, mentally, emotionally, and sometimes even physically depleting. It really can wear you out. Do yourself a favor and just refuse to argue about it.

In God's Defense

Some people think that to remain silent in the face of critical remarks about spiritual matters is simply wrong. They believe it is their duty to speak up with boldness when this kind of situation arises. Are they right about that? Should we speak out, or should we keep quiet when people make comments that contradict our faith?

The fact is that there's no universal answer for that question. Different situations require different responses. There isn't one response that will fit every situation. Sometimes it would be harmful to speak up, but at other times, taking a stand would be exactly the right response.

Remember this: You have the Spirit of Jesus Christ living inside you. The important thing to remember is that you don't have to *react* to anything that another person may say. You have the ability to *respond* when you have a clear internal sense of what to do. That is how you experience Spirit-led leadership. Do what you sense Him guiding you to do. If you don't sense what you need to do, take that as evidence that you are to say nothing. Remember that being silent when you aren't being led to speak is sometimes harder than speaking. Trust Him and keep quiet when that's the appropriate response.

Sometimes saying nothing is the most effective response you could possibly offer. Proverbs 29:11 (KJV) says, "A fool uttereth all his mind: but a wise man keepeth it in till afterwards." There is wisdom in restraining your thoughts at times when speaking would serve no good whatsoever.

So don't fall into the mistake of thinking that you must answer when a criticism is made. If you need to speak, words will come to your mind that you realize are fitting for the situation. They will be words that are constructive and useful to the conversation. If the words you are about to speak will only exacerbate the situation by enflaming emotions, remember that a wise person "keepeth it in" and doesn't spew words that make matters worse.

The best thing about the whole subject of standing up in God's defense is that He needs no defense. The idea reminds me of the story of a critic who stood in front of DaVinci's *Mona Lisa*. A guide at the Louvre overheard her caustic remarks about whether the woman in the picture was smiling or not smiling, about the eyes of the Mona Lisa, and other silly comments.

The guide approached her and quietly said, "Madam, you must realize the paintings here are no longer on trial. They have already been studied and professionally evaluated by experts who have spent their entire lives studying art. What hangs here has set the bar for every generation of artists to come. No, Madam, it is not the paintings that are on trial. It is you who are on trial."

God doesn't need a defense attorney. Being a witness to His goodness as our Father is one thing. Defending Him is another matter altogether.

There's a great story in Judges 6. God tells Gideon to tear down the altar of the false god Baal. When morning came and the people saw what Gideon had done, they came to Joash and demanded that he send out his son Gideon so they could kill him. Joash responded to their demand with great insight relevant to our discussion about defending God.

> Joash replied to the hostile crowd around him, "Are you going to plead Baal's cause? Are you trying to save him? Whoever fights for him shall be put to death by morning! If Baal really is a god, he can defend himself when someone breaks down his altar" (Judges 6:31 NIV).

The response of Joash was insightful and applicable to believers today. He essentially said, "If Baal really is a god, why does he need you to defend him? Can't he defend himself?"

The obvious answer is, of course, that the true God can defend Himself, and we flatter ourselves to think He needs us to do it. Somehow we have gotten the idea that God needs us to be His public defender, but the very idea is preposterous. The One who created humanity from mud isn't intimidated by the rants and raves of the ungrateful, and He doesn't need us to come to His defense.

You Decide How to Respond

Again, there is a proper time and place to bear witness to who we know our God to be. Remember, there is no universal application in this kind of situation. We must be sensitive to know the best response in each moment.

If your husband consistently tries to provoke you with offhanded comments about spiritual matters, learn to respond in an appropriate way. You have no control over what he will say, but you have complete control over how you will and will not respond. Begin responding now instead of reacting.

Stand firm in whatever way you respond without being emotionally shaken by what anybody else says about your faith or your God. Your Father lovingly holds in His arms those who say wrong things. Like a parent cuddling a misbehaving child, He patiently allows them to vent their pain and anger without reacting to their verbal tantrums. Instead, He patiently responds because He knows why people act the way they do and say the things they say. That insight makes Him the perfect parent!

Don't worry if your husband's language doesn't always reflect what you want to see in him from a spiritual standpoint. He, too, is on a journey, and the One who loves him will guide his steps across the rocky terrain until He brings him through to the pasture beside still waters.

Be patient. Wait and watch. Respond as Christ in you responds to him. In time, your trust and your Father's love will prevail.

14

Other Voices

estiny and Cody were in a difficult phase in their relationship. They became annoyed with each other over the slightest things. One day, he left the lawn mower in the driveway, so she couldn't park in the garage when she came home from work. One evening, she talked on the phone with her mother while the two of them sat together eating dinner.

Small things quickly became big things when either of them expressed even slight disapproval of whatever the other had done. Cody and Destiny were DINKs—a "double income, no kids" couple. They had been married for six years. They both had good jobs, so finances weren't a problem. There was no doubt in their minds that they loved each other. That wasn't the issue. The problem was that they couldn't be together for a whole evening without some sort of verbal skirmish over the simplest of things. It seemed inevitable that it would happen, even on evenings when Destiny told herself she would make an extra effort to keep things upbeat and avoid any disagreements. Nothing seemed to work.

One day toward the end of her workday, just before five, a couple of friends at work came to her desk. "A few of us are going to Barnaby's Grill to chill out when we leave today. Why don't you come with us?" Barnaby's was a cozy place, perfect for visiting together. In fact, she and Cody had eaten dinner together there several times.

Knowing Cody usually got home an hour after she did, Destiny agreed. She called their home phone and left a voice message that he would pick up when he got home. "Hey, it's me. A few of us are gonna stop by Barnaby's after work today, just to hang out for a little while. I should be home not long after you get this message."

Time flew when the four of them went to Barnaby's. They laughed and talked together until somebody noticed that it was already 6:15. Three of the ladies had husbands waiting at home, and all agreed that it had been fun but that they needed to get home.

When Destiny got home, Cody was on the couch, eating. "There's Chinese on the kitchen counter," he said to Destiny.

"Great, thanks," she answered.

"Have fun with the girls?" Cody asked in a noncritical way.

"Yeah, I really did. It was good to kick back and laugh a little after work."

"That's good," Cody answered.

And that was all that was said about it. Cody sat on the couch watching TV while Destiny sat on the love seat half-watching TV while playing Words with Friends on her iPhone. The evening passed without incident.

As the weeks passed, the girls began to visit Barnaby's more frequently together after work. Their schedule evolved into Tuesdays and Thursdays every week. Destiny enjoyed being with her friends, and the time spent together nurtured a growing personal relationship with all of them.

As the weeks passed, Destiny and her friends began to stay at Barnaby's until eight. Cody didn't seem to mind, and Destiny enjoyed the time out. As time passed, conversation among the girls had become increasingly personal.

Destiny learned that April and her husband had been having problems for quite some time and that she had recently filed for divorce. Janna seemed to have a fairly good relationship with her husband. Then there was Jen, the only single one of the bunch, who always had stories of her latest "man moments," which ranged from comments about somebody she flirted with to details of her most recent intimate encounter.

Destiny said nothing, but some of Jen's stories made her uncomfortable. Having been reared in a Christian family, Destiny thought that even though she and Cody might not have the perfect marriage and despite the fact that she had shared some of their problems with the group, Jen felt free to divulge a little too much information. But that's the way the dynamics of the group had evolved. Anybody felt free to say anything about any subject.

That freedom gradually became unhealthy for Destiny, although she hadn't recognized that fact. She found herself sharing more and more about the things that bothered her with Cody. Each time she told about something he had done to annoy her, the others responded quickly and harshly. They affirmed her, but they also talked about Cody in ways that bordered on mockery. Something didn't feel right about these times to Destiny, but she liked having her viewpoint validated by her friends' opinions.

As time passed, Destiny's complaints about Cody became more and more frequent. "What do you think I should do?" Destiny asked one day after she and Cody had an argument. Cody had just told her he was going on a weekend fishing trip, and the weekend was only two days away. Destiny thought it was wrong for him to wait until the last minute to share his plans with her. Cody didn't see the big deal. This was the first time she had actually asked for advice from the group, and each of the girls was ready to offer her input.

"Have you considered insisting to Cody that the two of you sit down and discuss it in a calm and rational way?" Janna asked. "It sounds as if you haven't actually had a real conversation about it yet."

April's advice was more direct: "Tell that man that you don't get to do things like that on the spur of the moment and that he won't either. If you stand for this now, you'll be dealing with it again and again in the days ahead."

"Forget that," Jen said. "I'm going to Cancun for the weekend on a two-night, three-day package I found online. Just go with me and we'll have fun!"

As things turned out, Destiny didn't take any of her friends' suggestions. She simply stayed home while Cody took his trip. However, something was changing inside her. An inner brooding was quietly doing its damage.

When I met Destiny, her marriage had been deteriorating quickly over the past year. As she shared the story I've told you, I began to see a pattern with Destiny's actions. The pattern involved her becoming angry with Cody, holding in her emotions with him, and venting them when she met with her friends. The outcome was always the same. Janna, April, and Jen always validated her feelings, and then they gave their own advice about how Destiny should respond.

Little by little, this destructive habit had poisoned Destiny's mind about the tension in her marriage. Her friends always affirmed that she was in the right and Cody was in the wrong, so Destiny had become blind to the growing distance between her and her husband. In every tense situation that came up between them, she believed she was justified in her feelings and correct in her thinking. There was no doubt that Cody was often in the wrong, but Destiny couldn't see that she was often wrong too. It wasn't a one-sided situation, and she was not without fault.

As time passed, Destiny began to ask her friends' advice more frequently, and they were quick to give it. Jen's advice often seemed too extreme, and Janna's was passive much of the time, but Destiny usually felt that what April told her was reasonable. April didn't sacrifice her own independence, but she didn't share Jen's more extreme mindset.

So April, who was still recovering from the sting of her own divorce, became the voice that carried the most weight with Destiny.

Little by little, her friend's opinion began to frame the way Destiny viewed her own marriage. The fact that April's thoughts were probably tainted by her own recent experiences didn't occur to Destiny. That hidden reality was having a negative effect in her thinking, and it was becoming more detrimental than Destiny realized.

April's gradual influence in Destiny's perspective on her own marriage was completely unhealthy. Remember me saying at the beginning that Destiny loved Cody? As time progressed, the resentment fueled by April's advice began to overshadow Destiny's feelings of love. Things were deteriorating because Destiny was listening to the wrong person say the wrong things.

Let's see how this situation may apply to your relationship with your own husband. It's normal to want to share your feelings with a friend, and there's certainly nothing inherently wrong with that. Many times, God uses our friends to help us when we hurt. The Bible says, "The heartfelt counsel of a friend is as sweet as perfume and incense" (Proverbs 27:9 NLT).

That doesn't mean, however, that just because you consider a person a friend, her words will be helpful to you. Sometimes a well-meaning friend may unintentionally give advice that will hurt you instead of help you. We can safely assume that April never intended to cause further damage in Destiny's relationship with Cody, but that's what was happening.

There are some things you need to keep in mind about listening to your friends' advice about your own marriage. Sincere advice from an unhealthy source can do serious damage to your relationship with your husband.

Choose Your Advisors Carefully

When it comes to medical issues, you wouldn't automatically accept the opinion of a friend simply because you have a good relationship with that person. If you needed financial counsel, you would be careful about whose input you took seriously. You would be selective about whose advice you would follow in these areas, and the same should be true about whom you talk with about the details of your marriage.

Destiny gravitated toward April's advice for the wrong reasons. April's opinions resonated with the pent-up anger Destiny was feeling. April's advice sounded right because it fit with Destiny's underlying emotions. It sounded reasonable because Destiny's objectivity was already skewed by resentment. April's advice was well intended but polluted by her own recent marital conflicts and divorce.

You may tend to open up to a sympathetic friend simply because she seems to understand your situation, but it is important to prayerfully consider whether you should share details about your most intimate relationship. Your relationship to your husband is a valuable gift from God, and you should treat it that way when you talk about it. Your Father may well have a friend in mind whom He wants to speak through to encourage and help you. But it is important to know who that person is and not to verbally purge about your situation to a friend simply because she seems to care.

Trust a Friend Who Builds You Up

Destiny believed that April understood the problem and could offer helpful advice because she had been through similar struggles with her ex-husband. In reality, April simply had taken up Destiny's offense with little objectivity about her situation. The fact that April's marriage had failed didn't automatically disqualify her from offering any help to Destiny. However, April had become jaded, and her advice consistently vindicated Destiny's negative feelings.

Remember that your heavenly Father is always interested in healing, restoring, reconciling, and making things right. When He is using a friend to help you, her advice will always have an underlying tone of redemption and hope. That doesn't mean that good advice never challenges one to stand firm or to make hard choices.

However, godly advice never nurtures resentment or bitterness. Advice that is truly good is saturated with grace.

G.K. Chesterton wrote, "The word 'good' has many meanings. For example, if a man were to shoot his grandmother at a range of five hundred yards, I should call him a good shot, but not necessarily a good man." Don't simply look for good advice. Look for godly advice.

The voice of godly advice will always be constructive, not destructive. It will encourage restoration, not deterioration. Sometimes a husband's misbehavior calls for an assertive stance, as we have discussed in earlier chapters, but the ultimate goal will always be healing. Godly advice will motivate you to seek restoration and not simply validate your thoughts and feelings about being right. Godly advice will facilitate rebuilding a relationship and not dismantling it.

Listen to the Voice Above All Others

You are God's child, so His Spirit lives inside you. That reality provides a greater resource than you may have imagined. He is ever present in your personal circumstances. He knows every detail about your marriage and every other aspect of your life. Equally as important, He cares!

As we have seen, the Bible says, "Unless the LORD builds a house, the work of the builders is wasted" (Psalm 127:1 NLT). God Himself wants to build up your marriage. His voice will speak to you and show you how to relate to your husband in a way that will benefit both of you. Do you listen for His voice? Are you as quick to share your concerns with Him as you are with a friend? Have you considered that He may want to speak directly to you and show you answers to your questions and concerns?

Jesus promised He would speak to us through His indwelling Spirit. "But when He, the Spirit of truth, comes, He will guide you into all the truth; for He will not speak on His own initiative, but whatever He hears, He will speak; and He will disclose to you what is to come" (John 16:13). The Spirit of God will tell you how to experience a strong relationship with your husband. Before you listen to other voices, open your heart and mind to hear His voice. He will teach you how to relate to your husband in a way that moves you toward the future God has in mind for you.

Pray about your marriage. Pray for your husband. Ask the One whose indwelling life defines you to help you see your husband and your marriage through His eyes. Resentment toward another person withers in the presence of consistent prayer for him.

Perhaps a need in your relationship to your husband requires some adjustment on your part. Are you listening to the wrong voices? Are you respecting the sacred covenant of your marriage by listening to the voice of the One who instituted marriage in the beginning?

It's fine to be encouraged by a God-given confidant, but avoid allowing your mind and emotions to be influenced by any voice that doesn't express the essence of Agape. His voice, the Holy Spirit, will speak health and wholeness into your marriage. Listen to Him, and your need to hear lesser voices will pale by comparison.

15

Clean Fights

*I*f you had more ambition, we'd be further along by now!" Emma angrily said to Mason. "I've told you to send out résumés, but you'd rather stay right where you are no matter what the best thing for us might be!"

"There you go again! Blame me when we come up short because you don't understand how to live within a budget. You *never* give one thought to whether or not we have the money for something. If it's in the bank, you assume it must be there to spend. Well, Emma, we have monthly bills that have to be paid out of that money!"

"You're the one who didn't pay last month's power bill! Now we owe two months instead of one. It's not like I've spent the money on something we don't need. If you'd acted with just a little responsibility we wouldn't be having this conversation!" Emma responded.

"Yeah, blame it on me," Mason continued. "That's a lot easier than admitting that you don't seem to understand that no matter how much money a family makes, there has to be a limit on what is being spent every month!"

Without another word, Emily turned and walked out of the room and into the kitchen. Mason stormed into his home office, slamming the door hard enough to make sure Emma heard it.

This kind of exchange takes place in homes all over the world every day. Arguing. I'm not talking about physical conflict. Most couples don't reach that stage in their disagreements, but many don't realize that speaking the wrong words may have irrevocable consequences.

Disagreements in marriage are universal. In fact, if a couple never disagrees, one person has probably become so passive that the marriage is on dangerous ground for altogether different reasons. Verbal disagreements are not only normal but can be healthy if they are expressed in the appropriate way. You can't live with a person and not have differences of opinion, but the way you handle those differences is of utmost importance.

Looking at the brief glimpse into the argument between Emma and Mason, we see several red flags about their communication skills and thus the health of their marriage. Read the description of their conversation again and note each of the mistakes you can identify in their disagreement. They did at least four or five things wrong. Can you see them?

Address Behavior, Not Character

Some of the things we say in an argument carry more weight than others. When we feel angry, we may be tempted to make the harshest statement we can think of. But doing that can cause long-term relational damage that is very, very hard to reverse. Angry words are one thing. Words that belittle the very essence of somebody's character are a more serious issue.

Emma's criticism that Mason had no ambition crossed the line. Married partners usually know each other's vulnerabilities and insecurities. To verbally strike in an area that diminishes your mate as a person is not only wrong but also may do lasting damage. Think of the areas in your own life in which you feel most insecure. When anybody gouges you in those areas of sensitivity, the effect is exaggerated, and the resulting damage isn't overcome easily. You don't want to do that to the man you love.

One wife said to me, "Well, he knows how I am and that I don't really mean it." No, he doesn't know you don't really mean it. In fact, a phantom voice inside him has already told him that what you said is true. When you affirm what that voice says, it's next to impossible for him to readily believe that you don't mean it. He may know that you love him, but your love won't soon overcome the damage done by words that fuel his insecurity.

Be careful what you say. Words can be like a shotgun blast. The loud noise subsides, but the damage is done. The Bible says, "The words of the reckless pierce like swords" (Proverbs 12:18 NIV).

Tell him what you don't like. Say it clearly and even firmly if you want, but make sure to talk about his behavior. Wrong actions can be changed in no time, but when a person is made to feel that he is inherently bad, his pain isn't easy to move past.

What are you to do if your husband attacks your character? First, don't *react* to such a thing. Instead, *respond* to his words. If your husband has a habit of saying angry words that diminish you as a person, those words probably push your buttons, making it difficult for you to answer in a healthy way. In fact, your reaction may almost seem involuntary when you feel provoked.

Instead of reacting, decide now how you will respond when he says something to you that is out of bounds. You could say something as simple as, "I'm not going to continue this conversation right now. You crossed the line by trying to reduce me as a person instead of talking about what I've done." Then, every time your husband commits this infraction, say the same words to him. If you will be consistent in this, he will learn that attacking your character won't help him make his point. It will only cause the conversation to end abruptly. To talk about bad behavior is acceptable, but to put somebody down crosses the line.

When you've ended a conversation in this way, let your emotions stabilize. Then, when the time is right, work together to set certain guidelines for how you will disagree with each other. Obviously, a big one will be that you don't belittle each other's character. Agree together to address actions and not go afoul by diminishing each other. Once you have agreed on the boundary lines for arguing, if your husband crosses a line in the future, stop at that moment and remind him that you've agreed not to go there. If he continues, end the conversation immediately. Later, when you've both settled down, come back to the discussion about how to disagree in a nondestructive way.

The idea of establishing these guidelines and agreeing about how to disagree may seem simple, but it works. You both have control over your words. "If a man thinks that he serves God, and does not hold his tongue, but deceives his heart, this person's service is worthless" (James 1:26 ABPE). Neither of you has to react. You can learn to hold your tongue and respond properly.

Avoid the Words "Never" and "Always"

Mason made a terrible choice by telling Emma, "You *never* give one thought to whether or not we have the money for something." When he made that statement, the discussion could no longer be about what was going on at the moment. Now it was much more than that. Mason had unwisely turned the conversation into something much bigger by using the word "never." His decision to use that word automatically and understandably put Emma on the defense. After all, now he wasn't just talking about one incident, but about an alleged habitual way of behaving.

When arguments occur, certain words usually do nothing but increase the emotional intensity of an already charged atmosphere. To say "you never" or "you always" is to throw gasoline on a fire. If your goal is to resolve the problem, avoid those phrases at all costs.

Also avoid statements that question your mate's intelligence.

Somebody might say, "What were you thinking?" or "That's insane!" but the other person is likely to hear, "You are stupid!" Questions and remarks like these don't serve a useful purpose. Avoid saying anything that could be construed as a veiled insult.

Making generalized accusations when arguing is harmful too. What we are feeling at the moment may seem like the way we feel all the time, but that often is not the case. It is easy to project the negative emotions of one intense situation into all of life. For example, your husband may not have done the yard work he said he would do today, but that doesn't warrant calling him lazy. The problem with volatile emotions during an argument is that our minds tend to quickly scan the other person's history and build a case that it's always like this. The accusations are never helpful and rarely even true.

It's important to avoid enflaming the argument by saying things that move away from the matter at hand and turn it into something much bigger. Stay focused on the details of this particular incident and speak rationally and calmly. Don't let it get out of hand and turn into something else.

Strive for Understanding, Not for Victory

Have you been married long enough to discover that even if you win an argument, you haven't necessarily won anything? Mature people realize that resolving differences isn't about being proven right. The goal is to understand and be understood. Most arguments stem from a lack of understanding by one or both partners.

Your husband may see things in a way that makes no sense to you whatsoever. Rather than immediately trying to prove that his way of seeing the matter is wrong, what might happen if you tried to understand *why* he sees it that way? Chances are that once you understood why he sees it the way he does, you can much more easily move toward a mutually agreeable solution.

Rather than immediately making assertions, determine to ask

questions. Avoid questions that are thinly veiled attempts to support your view, and think of sincere questions that build understanding. If your husband isn't normally a highly irrational person who has no acquaintance with common sense and ordinary logic, why not take the time to try to understand how he has reached his opinion?

Begin by seeking to understand before you try to be understood. Having first shown your husband the courtesy of actively listening to his perspective, you can then ask that he extend the same courtesy to you as you share your opinion. Gaining a personal victory by proving your point isn't the aim. Understanding is the bedrock of conflict resolution in any situation, including marriage.

Once your husband realizes that you understand his viewpoint, you will be in a better position to present your own viewpoint. People tend to not listen if they feel they haven't been heard. That's why it is important to demonstrate that you understand his view. Understanding doesn't necessitate that you agree, but only that you have grasped what he is saying.

Before you begin to explain your position, ask him, "Do you feel like I've heard and understood you?" If he doesn't, ask him to say more about what he believes you haven't gotten yet. Calmly talk it through until he acknowledges that he feels heard and understood.

When it is your time to speak, choose to speak calmly without emotionally charged words. If he interrupts, stop him and ask for the courtesy of allowing you to complete your thoughts before interjecting his response. Remind him that you did the same for him. These guidelines for arguing apply to any situation where people disagree with each other.

Dealing with Bickering

Some couples seem to bicker with each other constantly. Sometimes the arguments are over the silliest things. Marriage is not supposed to be that way. If you find yourself repeatedly bickering with your husband over insignificant things, chances are that those things are not the real sources of the problem. When there's always a short fuse between you, it's important to discover what is causing you both to live in such an emotionally volatile relationship.

Sometimes stress may be the cause. When couples face trying circumstances, it's easier to be impatient with each other than with anybody else. After keeping our emotions in check all day, we commonly let our guard down at home and finally release those negative feelings. When we snap at each other and know that it's because we're handling stress inappropriately, the easiest and most direct route to resolution is a simply apology. "I'm sorry. I'm feeling uptight right now, but I don't want to take it out on you. Will you forgive me?" Sharing those words with each other can add warmth to what might have been a bleak evening for you both.

Sometimes we constantly bicker because we have fallen into a rut of misbehavior. One person repeatedly does something that irritates the other. Each time, the other person reacts in the same way as before. The first person then reacts in another well-established way, and on it goes. The results are always the same.

As the old saying goes, "Insanity is doing the same thing over and over and expecting different results." Again, the answer here is communication. Talk about it together. Change what is within your power to change. Find a way to compromise. Agree together that the behavior that triggers the incident isn't worth the fallout. Seek out a new approach.

Another cause for constant bickering is pride. We may be inclined to see the fault in our mate while being blind to our own responsibility in the situation. Your husband may indeed behave poorly, but that doesn't negate the possibility that you are contributing to the problem.

My wife, Melanie, and I married when we were 19 and 18, respectively. Two years later we had our first child, and within seven years we had four children. Needless to say, stress levels were high for such a young couple. As is often the case in such scenarios, we found ourselves bickering often. No matter how determined we both were to avoid arguments, they would break out over the silliest things. It was not pleasant.

I was blind to the part I was playing, but I did have enough understanding from my Christian upbringing to know that praying about the problem was wise. However, I didn't have enough wisdom to know *what* to pray. So my private prayer every day was that God would open Melanie's eyes to her wrong thinking and actions. "You have to change her, Lord!"

We laugh about it now, but I was serious at the time. After praying this way for some time, I sensed my Father speaking to me one night. I will never forget it. His words arose in my consciousness as clearly as if they had been audible: "Steve, I want to change *you.*"

I was stunned. In my pride, it hadn't occurred to me that *I* might need to change. That simply wasn't on my radar, but I heard Him. I knew it was His voice. So I began to pray about my attitude and my actions. I still didn't think Melanie was without any fault, but I didn't focus on her need for change. I focused on allowing God's Spirit to transform me, and He did.

I began to treat my wife in a loving way. I began to act and react toward her like a husband who was following Christ. I changed, and she saw it. When she did, something amazing happened. She changed too.

Your husband may be the one in the wrong. You may be justified in feeling the way you do, but has it helped the situation? What might happen if you were to take the initiative to bring about change? What could take place if you laid down your pride, setting aside the issue of who is right and who is wrong, and simply responded to your husband in undeserved grace?

Your husband may need to learn appropriate behavior, but your Father may intend to teach him through your actions. The Bible teaches that the behavior of a wife can have a profound effect in changing her husband (1 Corinthians 7:14; 1 Peter 3:1-2). You've been waiting for him to change, but your Father may want to first change you.

Arguing is normal in any marriage. The question is, will you and your husband argue constructively? Allow the Holy Spirit to teach you how to "be angry, and yet do not sin" (Ephesians 4:26). Wives who walk in grace sometimes argue with their husbands, but they have learned how to do it properly.

Juggling Acts

I feel like I'm a failure most of the time," Rebecca said. "Between work, church involvement, the boys' ball games, my daughter's dance lessons, housework, time with my husband, and maintaining a few friendships, I feel like I'm doing everything in my life halfway. Instead of doing a good job at anything, I feel like I'm doing a terrible job at everything!"

"How have you tried to deal with the stress of all this thus far?" I asked.

"I've tried everything I know to do," she answered. "I've lived from a to-do list, read articles online about time management, prayed for God's help to get it all done…I don't know what else to do," she answered with a slight quiver in her voice. "I feel like a failure as a wife, a mother, a friend…even as a Christian."

Rebecca isn't the only wife I've counseled through the years who has expressed these frustrations. In today's culture, where women hold themselves to so many expectations, most feel frazzled if not completely frantic about all the demands. There are only 24 hours in a day, and nobody can do anything to change that. Many wives feel there just isn't time to do everything that must be done.

In addition to the mental and emotional frustrations associated with the unrelenting demands of life, a woman's physical body also responds to the stress. Cortisol is a hormone produced by the adrenal glands. It helps you to effectively deal with normal challenges of the day by giving you that extra boost you need. The adrenals also produce another energy hormone called DHEA. When stress becomes a chronic problem, the body maintains a high cortisol production while the DHEA levels drop. When that happens, the energy level drops, and fatigue comes on quickly and won't go away.

So there you have it. Most wives are mentally, emotionally, and physically exhausted! That doesn't solve your problem, but it at least should help you realize you're not alone.

Show Yourself Grace

How are you to juggle so many responsibilities at one time? It is important that you understand one thing immediately. *You are normal.* Every wife I've talked to about this problem has struggled with a sense of guilt to some degree. Each one, without exception, has believed that she is at fault for not handling things better.

You may feel as if others have a better handle on this and seem to be able to get it all done more successfully than you do. But remember this: You don't know what *they're* thinking and feeling. Chances are that the person you admire—the one who seems to manage all the details of life—is struggling with the same kind of frustration that you have.

So here's a starting point: Show yourself some grace. Stop allowing yourself to think that other wives are admirable successes in this area and that you are a dismal failure. Stop comparing yourself to other people—period.

The apostle Paul described some people who were evaluating their own personal worth. "They are only comparing themselves with each other, using themselves as the standard of measurement. How ignorant!" (2 Corinthians 10:12 NLT). Paul makes it clear that comparing yourself with other people is foolish and harmful. It can only lead to two places—both of them bad.

First, if you perceive that someone is doing better than you, you will feel diminished by her superior performance. You'll likely find yourself wondering why you can't be more like her. You will compare her strengths to your weaknesses, which is always counterproductive. Second, if you think you are doing better than someone, you may feel prideful. Instead of feeling inferior, you may feel superior and judgmental. Needless to say, a prideful attitude is never helpful either.

Most wives respond the first way. They feel that they don't measure up. The wise approach is to avoid comparison altogether. Even if another person seems to be managing a perfect balance in life, her lifestyle isn't yours. You are a unique person in circumstances that aren't exactly like anybody else's, so there's no benefit in comparing yourself to anybody else. The Bible calls such comparisons ignorant.

Seek Cooperation from Your Family

In the past, life really was simpler. Society didn't have as many options for how we spent our time. We weren't torn in many directions the way we are today. Decades ago, personal responsibilities were defined by gender much more than they are now. Watch some of the old TV programs from the '50s, and you'll get a fairly accurate picture of what life was like in those days. The number of women in the labor force was around 30 percent then. Today 70 percent of women in the United States work outside the home.

The challenge for wives today is that many of the older assumptions about roles at home remain, but wives have assumed much more responsibility. I won't presume to prescribe which household responsibilities are appropriate for wives and which are appropriate for husbands. But clearly, women who have joined the labor force and also continued to keep things running smoothly at home are carrying more responsibilities than their mothers and grandmothers did. In other words, your workload is heavier than your grandmother's probably was. Even setting aside careers outside the home, today's busy culture brings its own increasing demands.

When a workload significantly changes, there must be an accompanying transition in the workforce to avoid a problem. In other words, something has to give. Wives' gradually increasing responsibilities through the years have reached a tipping point that demands attention. This is especially true if you're among the 70 percent who work outside the home.

The point is that you may need help. I have counseled many wives through the years who were trying to shoulder the responsibilities of their careers, household duties, children, church, social lives, and marriage with little or no support at home. Some of them had prayed repeatedly for God to give them the strength to do all these things. They didn't realize that He never intended for them to carry the whole load alone.

Even Jesus had 12 disciples who helped Him fulfill the ministry His Father had given Him to do. Perhaps it's time for you to sit down with your family and discuss sharing the load—even if your children are small. There are things they can learn to do at an early age. This will not only help ease the routine at home but also prepare them to live productively in society in the days ahead.

What role does your husband assume at home? If you have equal duties outside the home, you need to have an equitable distribution of duties in the home. Some wives have half-jokingly said that they have never found their husbands to be more desirable than when they are sharing household responsibilities. It's a matter of shared respect and expressing love in meaningful ways. Is this a discussion you need to have together?

Learn to Live with Imperfection

We all have an ideal in mind concerning the things we do in life. We have been taught to be conscientious about what we do and to strive for excellence. Certainly, nothing is wrong with that philosophy of living. It is admirable and serves as a good baseline for everything we do.

There is, however, a difference between being conscientious and being a perfectionist. A person can be conscientious and recognize a job well done without needing it to be perfect. Perfectionists always see the shortcomings in a finished task, even if they are so insignificant that nobody else would even notice.

Sometimes wives need to assess their capabilities and adjust their ideals to more realistic levels. Things can be good, even excellent, without being perfect. Learning to live with less than perfect results is important for peace of mind because nobody ever achieves perfection.

God doesn't expect you to live a perfect lifestyle. The psalmist wrote, "For He Himself knows our frame; He is mindful that we are but dust" (Psalm 103:14). To put it another way, God knows that you are only human. Do you know that, or do you place expectations on yourself to be superhuman and then feel frustrated when you see that you aren't?

A wife walking in grace finds fulfillment in having done her best considering the limitations that life imposes on her. When God finished creating, He looked at what He had done and said, "It is good." He wants you to be able to say the same about what you do. In fact, to be able to say so is a godly quality.

Does it really matter if some things go undone or are postponed? Is it worth sacrificing peace of mind, emotional stability, and physical well-being in order to accomplish it all? Does it really matter that much in the big picture? These questions merit serious consideration.

Learning to live with results that are less than perfect may be an acquired skill that the Holy Spirit wants to teach you. The next time you look at a finished job and are tempted to nitpick and judge it through the lens of perfectionism, don't be surprised if you hear Him say, "Let it go. It is good." When you hear that still, small voice, listen and do it. In the long run, you will discover the grace of fulfillment instead of the guilt of self-imposed standards that condemn you.

Hit the Delete Button

If you want to walk in grace, then grace needs to be the governing force in your daily lifestyle. Grace is not demanding. To the contrary, it is inspiring. It is not judgmental. Instead, it is affirming. Grace lifts you up. It doesn't wear you down.

So in light of these observations about grace, you may need to ask yourself whether grace is governing your daily lifestyle. It is normal to feel tired at times. It is sometimes necessary to give for a time beyond what we might be able to give constantly, but if you are worn out all the time, something needs to change.

Jesus said, "Walk with me and work with me—watch how I do it. Learn the unforced rhythms of grace. I won't lay anything heavy or ill-fitting on you. Keep company with me and you'll learn to live freely and lightly" (Matthew 11:29-30 MSG). That promise isn't restricted to just one part of your life. He wants you to see how His grace can permeate you and everything you do.

Grace leads you to your place of excellence by showing you what God has designed for you and then empowering you to do those things. A legalistic mind imposes additional expectations and duties that God never initiated. He will empower and enable you to do the things He has for you, not the things He never intended you to do.

So if you are constantly praying for strength but continuing to experience frustration and dissatisfaction, stop and consider things for a moment. Are you trying to do more than He has asked of you? If so, you're on an endless treadmill that will never bring you fulfillment or peace.

It may seem at first glance that there is nothing in your routine that you can set aside, but that isn't necessarily the case. Pray about this issue. Ask Him to show you the things that aren't part of His design for your lifestyle. You can be assured He hasn't called you to burnout. He intends for you to continue burning brightly, and that will happen only if you're doing what He intends for you to do by the power of His indwelling life.

You have to make this decision. Others can't do it for you regardless of how sincere they may be. Your path is one that your Father and you must work out. Yes, life can be challenging at times, but when duties are demanding *all the time*, that should be a red flag that you can recognize.

How can you restructure your lifestyle and live in "the unforced rhythms of grace"? Maybe the answer involves hitting the delete button on some things. If you ask and trust Him, the Holy Spirit will show you the weights in life that you may need to let go. You may hear a voice inside you arguing, "But this is a good thing!" That may be true, but not every good thing is a God-thing. You are called to do some things but not everything. Just because you *can* do it doesn't mean you are *supposed* to do it.

Some people, even family members, may protest your decision to hit the delete button when they are affected. In particular, giving up responsibilities at church may provoke that sort of response. If so, stand strong in faith that you are following your Father's leadership in your grace walk. Don't allow pressure, manipulation, or guilt from others to cause you to forfeit the joy of walking the path He has prepared for you. You have one life in this world. Live it the way He intends. That's not selfish. It's the way of obedience and faith.

The majority of wives today are juggling the duties they have accepted and struggling to keep everything going. Remember this: Jugglers work in a circus because their ability is so unusual. The rarity of their skill is what makes them notable.

The grace walk isn't a circus, and you aren't called to amaze people by the way you can juggle everything you pick up. You are called to handle certain things with unforced rhythms of grace. Don't settle for anything less. Doing more than your Father intends you to do may bring the applause of others, but it saddens the One who loves you most. It saddens Him because He wants you to know the joy of trusting Him and simply doing what He has called you to do in the power of His indwelling Spirit.

Prodigal Sons

Shane has been a leader in his church for almost 15 years. Teresa leads a ladies' Bible study that meets once a week. They have been involved in practically every ministry the church has had in the time they have attended there. They are well respected among their friends both inside and outside the church.

Their two children, Abby and Lane, grew up in the church. At home they both learned how to live in a way that honors Christ. Abby is a senior in high school, and Lane is in his third year at the state university three hours from home. Abby has always behaved well and never given Shane and Teresa any problems. The same was true of Lane until his sophomore year away at school.

Shane and Teresa began to see a gradual change in him during that second year away from home. His attitude remained respectful toward them when he came home on weekends, but he seemed more withdrawn. His parents noticed that his comments about various topics seemed to reflect an underlying attitude of rebellion toward most of the things he had been taught all his life, including matters of faith.

At first, Shane and Teresa assured each other that Lane was simply trying to find his own voice. He was away from home, and it made sense that he needed to establish his own personhood in his own mind. With more than a little apprehension, they hoped and tried to believe that he was fine and that he wouldn't veer far from the core values they had taught him.

As he approached the end of his second year away, Lane's visits home on the weekends became less and less frequent. He typically explained that there was a social activity of one sort or another that was happening on campus and that he was going to stay there for the weekend. Shane and Teresa recognized that this was a normal aspect of the transition from youth to adulthood that happens when a young man attends school. Again, they tried to encourage each other not to be overly concerned about the changes they saw.

One weekend when Lane came home to celebrate Abby's birthday with the family, things changed in an instant. Teresa was in his bedroom to gather up the laundry he had brought home from school so she could wash it for him. She knew he normally brought it home in a duffel bag that was there on the bed, so she picked up the bag to take it to the laundry room.

Glancing down at the foot of the bed, she noticed his overstuffed backpack. Assuming that more laundry may be in it, she unzipped it and found she was right. T-shirts were stuffed inside. She pulled them out and then reached into the bottom of the bag to make sure she was leaving nothing behind. Feeling something that made her curious, she discovered a small sandwich bag half filled with marijuana. In that moment, Teresa's suppressed fears were confirmed.

She put the bag back into the backpack and for the rest of the afternoon agonized over how to handle the situation. When Shane arrived home from a men's meeting at church, she asked him to come into their bedroom and told him what she had found. They both were emotionally devastated, but after discussing it, they agreed that they needed to talk to Lane about it.

That evening, when Abby went to see a movie with friends, they asked Lane to come into the den so they could talk. They confronted him about what Teresa had discovered, but to their surprise, Lane showed no remorse. To the contrary, he defended having the marijuana and insisted that it was no big deal. He spoke aggressively about how he didn't smoke it that often and insisted that he could stop it anytime he wanted. He almost took a preaching tone as he described how he had read that pot didn't have the addictive pull on people that some think it does. "It's no worse than having a glass of wine," he insisted.

Lane went back to the university campus on Sunday afternoon. Shane and Teresa hugged him, and everybody tried to act normal, but they all felt the underlying heaviness of the situation. "Take care of yourself," Shane softly spoke as he hugged his son.

"Don't worry, Dad. I'm fine," Lane responded.

As the weeks passed, Shane and Teresa wrestled with fear. "Marijuana is a stepping-stone to other drugs a lot of the time," Teresa said to Shane one evening with tears in her eyes.

"I know," Shane answered, "but there's nothing we can do other than entrust him to the Lord now. What he does now is up to him, not us anymore."

Less than two months later, the phone rang around ten o'clock one Saturday evening. Teresa answered and heard Lane's trembling voice: "Mom, can I speak to Dad?"

"Is everything okay, Lane?" she asked.

"I'm fine. Please, can I speak to Dad?"

She handed Shane the phone and watched as he stood in silence listening to Lane for a few moments. After what seemed like forever, Shane finally spoke: "We'll be there in a few hours."

He hung up the phone and looked at Teresa. "What is it?" she asked with obvious panic in her voice.

"It's a DUI. He said he was at a sports bar with friends watching a ball game on TV and had a few beers. When he was driving back to campus, he was stopped and arrested."

Teresa began to cry hard. Shane tried to blink away his own tears as he held his wife in his arms without saying a word. Yes, things had changed. This traditional Christian couple had just been thrown into what felt like utter darkness.

Many Christian families live out scenarios like this. The circumstances may not be exactly the same, but the underlying issue is. A Christian couple rears their son with a sincere and committed determination to ground him in the faith so he will be prepared to face the world and live out his life in a way that honors God. They teach their daughter biblical truths. They pray with her at home. They take her to church. They seek to sincerely live out their faith in order to be examples. They hope and believe that their children will remain true to the things they have taught and practiced. Then the whole dream comes crashing down in what seems like a horrible nightmare come true.

There may not be a greater trial of faith than to see your children make choices that violate everything you have sought to teach them. It is a wrenching experience that can leave you feeling emotionally devastated, mentally confused, and physically exhausted. What do you do when you "train up a child in the way he should go" only to see him "depart from it"? Christian parents struggle to answer that question every day.

The Toxic Question

When a child consciously chooses to move away from the faith and lifestyle his parents have so earnestly sought to instill in him, the parents always ask the same toxic question: Why? It is important to quickly answer the question and then put it away.

Parents never cradle their young babies in their arms and imagine that one day those children will make choices that will break their hearts. Parents want their children to mature into responsible adults who make wise choices and find increasing success and fulfillment as they move through life.

So after spending your child's lifetime hoping and striving and praying for that outcome, how do you possibly find sense in it when it all seems to jump track and your child's life appears to be on a collision course with disaster? The answer is that *you can't make sense of it.* You will drive yourself to despair if you allow the question of why to continue to control you.

This is a trial in life that may likely never produce a satisfying, rational answer to the question of why. You will discover the way toward peace only by answering a different question: Who? Who is ultimately in control here? Not you—that's self-evident at this point. Only as we cast ourselves on God's unfailing faithfulness in the valleys of life will peace gradually begin to stabilize us in this situation. When you are asking why, here's the answer: "I don't know, but my Father knows, and I will trust Him in this dark place."

Affirming Your Role

Teresa asked Shane another question that every parent in this situation eventually asks: What did we do wrong? Once your child becomes old enough to make independent decisions over which you have no control, it is important to understand the answer to that question. There *is* an answer, and although it doesn't take away the pain, it will give you comfort if you believe it and embrace it. The answer is that you have done nothing wrong.

Regarding our children, the Bible says, "Bring them up in the discipline and instruction of the Lord" (Ephesians 6:4). Once you have done that, you have fulfilled your God-given responsibility. Don't scrutinize or judge yourself to determine whether you have failed.

Your role as a parent has never been to live out your child's life. What could you have done to *make her* make the right decision? Nothing. That is not your job. Your job is to teach her the right decision, and if you have done that, there is nothing more you could have done.

If your child has made wrong choices, it is important that you not waste yourself trying to identify what you've done wrong. To the contrary, affirm to yourself that you taught your child the choice Christ would have him make. You brought him up in the discipleship and teaching of the Lord. Having done that, you succeeded in your role. You may not feel as if that's true, but you must recognize that it is—unless you accept the delusion that you could control the choices your adult child would make.

Find Your Emotional Equilibrium

When children make destructive choices, parents have the impulse to rush in and change their course. The reality is, that isn't possible. You can pray for your child. You can encourage him. You can love her. You can be an example. You can even warn, but you cannot cause your child to make the appropriate decision once he is old enough to decide for himself.

Watching your son or daughter continue to make the wrong choice will knock you off balance emotionally like few things will. You can't continue to live in that emotional state day after day after day. It will destroy your emotional and mental health and can even affect your physical well-being.

What do you do? You take an emotional step backward. You consciously *choose* not to be held an emotional hostage by your child's behavior. That may mean that you decide to stop asking questions. What good does it do to discover tormenting answers over which you have no control? To step back may mean that you allow your child to suffer the consequences of the wrong choices. Teresa and Shane chose to allow Lane to go to court alone. He had to pay a heavy fine, attend a DUI school, and give up his driver's license for months. Teresa and Shane wisely chose not to allow Lane to be spared the consequences of his decisions.

This stepping back approach may feel as if you're indicating you don't care, but nothing could be further from the truth. Your child must learn, and God is skilled in using personal failure and pain to teach His children. Don't interfere with Him by trying to protect your child. You will only ensure that he doesn't learn the lesson his heavenly Father wants him to learn and thus is doomed to repeat the same failure again.

Love your child enough to let God work in the pain when it comes. Until then take the logistical actions necessary to maintain your own emotional equilibrium. This is a step of faith. If you don't believe it, just try it!

God Is Always at Work

As you wait, pray, and hope that your child will come to her senses, it is important to cling to the reality that God isn't finished with her. He loves your daughter infinitely more than you ever could. He sees where she is, and He cares. Our loving Father never abandons any of us in the midst of our foolishness. *His grace is bigger than our wrong choices.*

The psalmist wrote, "I would have despaired unless I had believed that I would see the goodness of the LORD in the land of the living" (Psalm 27:13). Hold on to that same belief. Our God is a good God. Trust Him with your child. Even though you aren't able to supervise your child's behavior, the sovereign God of the universe is watching over her. Our finite human minds wonder why He allows our children to go into the far country, but you can be assured that they don't go alone. He goes with them and promises to never leave or forsake them.

Nobody can outrun God's goodness or out-sin His grace. "Goodness and mercy shall *follow me* all the days of my life" (Psalm 23:6 KJV). Your Father is working in your child's life, even in the darkest moments.

Don't despair and don't lose hope. "Weeping may last through the night, but joy comes with the morning" (Psalm 30:5 NLT). The night may seem long, but the sun will shine again. Until then, wait on the Lord in faith and answer negative feelings with an affirmation of His loving-kindness. In the end, it will be clear that grace has won.

Blended Families

Tanya and Cory married four years ago. Tanya's daughter was nine and her son and stepson were both eleven. She had been divorced for a year and Cory had been divorced for six months when they began to date. It didn't take long until they both knew things were becoming serious between them.

They sincerely wanted things to work out well, not only with the two of them but with their children as well. They agreed to take their time allowing the children to become close. They went on outings with the three children almost every weekend. The kids seemed to enjoy being together.

Cory and Tanya didn't spend the night together until they were married. Tanya's divorce had been particularly hard, and it was very important to her that her children make the transition as easily as possible. She read books about second marriages and about blending two families together.

She and Cory went to great lengths to give loving time and attention to each other's children. They dated for three years before marrying to make sure the step would work well with the children. When they set their wedding date, they sat down with them and explained in a positive way that they were going to marry, describing how wonderful it would be when they all would become one happy family. The children all responded positively.

About six months into the marriage, it began to be apparent that the new arrangement wasn't working out as smoothly as they had hoped. Tanya's children were performing poorly at school, and they distanced themselves from Cory once the novelty of their new family had worn off. Cory's son, Troy, had shouted at Tanya one day when she had mildly corrected him for something he had done wrong. "You're not my mother!" he had said.

She and Cory prayed together that God would bring their blended family together as one, but things didn't seem to be unfolding that way. There were daily challenges that neither of them had anticipated. They were both confident that they made the right choice to marry, but the process of finding the right flow of life at home wasn't as natural as they had hoped.

Their family is a microcosm of society as a whole. Seventy-five percent of those who divorce ultimately remarry, and of those, 65 percent involve children from previous marriages. These new couples bring their own expectations of what the blended family will look like into the relationship. Most assume their new family will function with the same dynamics they have known in the past. When it doesn't work out that way (and it seldom does), the parents often become frustrated. That frustration sometimes increases until it affects the way they relate to the children and each other. These couples probably all came into the marriages believing they were the perfect candidates for a blended family, not expecting that it would be so difficult to adjust. Consequently, 60 percent of second marriages end in divorce. That statistic makes it very important that these couples find what works for them.

Preparations to Consider

Approaches to parenting aren't exactly the same from family to family. The ways you and others raise children will probably be similar in many general ways, but the specific day-to-day details will not be the same. This is an important thing for couples to discuss when they have children and are planning to marry.

It isn't possible to identify every scenario and plan a parenting strategy, but you can discuss and agree on some things before marrying. Don't leave every detail to a trial-and-error process that begins after you marry and the children are all living together. Rearing children from two family backgrounds requires a customized approach to parenting.

Where do you each set boundaries with the children? Have you agreed on bedtimes? What responsibilities in the household are age appropriate for the children? How will you handle discipline? What television programs, movies, and video games are okay? Don't wait until the children pull out a DVD to find out whether you are in agreement. Privately discuss items like these together before they become issues with the children. You may need to compromise if you have had different guidelines for various parenting matters. Begin implementing these guidelines before you are married to make the transition as smooth as possible.

Invest Heavily in the Children

Starting a new family together can be a real challenge for children. It will be important to invest much time and attention in their lives, especially in the beginning. Chances are that they may feel some jealousy about their parent marrying somebody else. They may also be jealous about other children vying for your attention.

Learning the dynamics of the new relationships among you can be a complex matter for everybody. It's true that love never fails, so be sure to lavish love on each one even as you require appropriate respect from them all.

You probably won't instantly develop intense feelings of love for your mate's children. Remember that nothing is hypocritical about showing love even when you don't feel the accompanying emotions. Don't judge yourself if your feelings for your stepchildren don't match the feelings you have for your own children. To make that comparison is to misunderstand the way your love for your stepchildren is going to grow. The point is not to love them all the same, but to love them all sincerely.

The younger the children are when you marry, the easier it will be for your family to feel like a biological family. If you marry somebody with a 14-year-old, it is unrealistic to think the transition will happen quickly. The fact that your feeling of love for your stepchildren is different doesn't mean you don't love them. Your love for his children will grow as they respond to your love.

The Bible refers to the apostle John as "the disciple whom Jesus loved." Why is he given that distinction in Scripture? I suspect it is for two reasons. First, John showed a greater capacity to receive the love of Jesus than did the others. He sat closer to Jesus than the others and even leaned back on Jesus (John 13:23,25). When Mary Magdalene told Peter and John about the empty tomb, John outran Peter to the tomb (John 20:4). John simply seemed to respond to the love of Jesus more readily than the other disciples. Your stepchild will respond too because "love never fails" (1 Corinthians 13:8).

Maybe your stepchild will seem needy. Use that as an opportunity to shower love. If the child acts aloof and doesn't respond to your expressions of love, don't withdraw affection. Pray to find the right balance and show affection anyway. Give the child space but understand that affectionate love is like a medicine and will nurture a relationship even if it grows more slowly than you might like. Be patient and just love.

The other reason John is called "the disciple whom Jesus loved" is simple. John called himself that in the Gospel he wrote! John couldn't get over the fact that Jesus loved *him*! As you lavish love on your stepchildren just as you do your biological children, they will respond. Human beings' greatest need is to be loved. Be consistent. They *will* eventually respond.

Discipline

When it comes to discipline, it may be helpful to allow the biological parent to lead the way in the beginning. Instantly taking an authoritarian role with each other's children may not produce the best results. The children will be much more willing to accept correction once they fully realize their stepparent loves them, but coming to this place is a process. It's not something that happens simply because the wedding has occurred.

Some parents are stricter disciplinarians than others, but to turn a simple act of correction into a power struggle with a child serves no helpful purpose. When correcting each other's child, have the child's biological parent affirm and support the stepparent's right to discipline until the child gets the message. Stand together in unity as parents. Don't allow the children to divide and conquer by pitting you against each other.

When you discipline the children, do it with a firm but loving demeanor. Do not bring correction in anger. This transition into a new family is difficult for the children. Divorce has already turned their emotional world upside down. The one constant they need in every situation now is love. Actively loving them will nurture a sense of security and safety in their new home, and right now they need all the security they can get.

The apostle Paul wrote that when training and instructing children in the Lord, you should not exasperate them (Ephesians 6:4 NIV). There is a way to correct children that builds them up and a way that tears them down. Be sure that correction at home is constructive in the life of the child and not emotionally destructive. The way to do that is to ensure that the prevailing tone is love throughout the entire process.

Faith as the Foundation

Many families make a false distinction between their everyday lives and their spiritual lives. Some families who would never think of missing a Sunday at church rarely mention Jesus Christ at home. Allowing that artificial distinction to exist is potentially devastating. You, your husband, and your children must understand that faith in Christ isn't just a part of your family life. They need to know that Christ *is* your life. It is from that relationship that everything else finds its meaning.

Through Moses, God instructed the Israelites to teach their children about Him.

> Fix these words of mine in your hearts and minds; tie them as symbols on your hands and bind them on your foreheads. Teach them to your children, talking about them when you sit at home and when you walk along the road, when you lie down and when you get up. Write them on the doorframes of your houses and on your gates, so that your days and the days of your children may be many in the land the LORD swore to give your ancestors, as many as the days that the heavens are above the earth (Deuteronomy 11:18-21 NIV).

God was telling the people to make sure His instruction was commonplace in daily life. Faith in Him wasn't to be discussed only in the synagogue. Talk about it when you are sitting at home, when you are out and about town, before you go to bed, while you're eating breakfast. Make your relationship to your Creator such an embedded, intimate part of your family life that your children will always see their faith as part of their normal daily living. Teach them to see it as the foundation of their lives each day.

The worst thing you can do in your family is to segregate your faith walk from your daily lifestyle. They are the same! Integrate your walk with Christ into every aspect of your lives at home and outside of home. Moses told the people why they needed to do this: "so that your days and the days of your children may be many in the land the LORD swore to give your ancestors." In new-covenant terminology, we may say that to teach your children that Christ is the very fabric of your family is to ensure that both now and in the days ahead you will enjoy the abundant life of grace that is your birthright in Jesus Christ.

Let Jesus Christ live His life through you. Don't become merely a religious family who says grace before meals, attends church, and mentions God from time to time. As a blended family, you have the opportunity to demonstrate that God can bring life out of death. The death of one marriage through divorce doesn't have to be the end of the story.

Give your new family to Him and recognize Him as the source and substance of your family identity. Act with grace in your marriage and with the children. Give wide margin to each other to make mistakes as you each learn the dynamics of living together. God wants to bless the new creation of your family and make Himself at home in you. Create a loving environment where everybody feels heard, everybody feels valued, and everybody is validated for who he or she is as a person. Nurture a home environment free of judgment and condemnation by loving profusely even when you don't agree or when correction is necessary. Be generous with praise and encouragement and scarce with criticism and short-tempered words. Honor each other by offering sincere compliments, by asking advice as well as giving it, by putting the other's desires above your own, by recognizing that children have opinions about family matters, and by sincerely listening to and showing respect for those opinions.

As a couple, honor each other in the presence of the children. Allow them to see the love you have for each other. Let them hear you talk about the way your faith and the presence of Christ affect your everyday lives. Pray in their presence. Act with integrity that they might learn it. Avoid language you wouldn't want them to use. Set an example of speaking graciously about other people and never commenting on the negative qualities you see in others. The list could go on.

Impossible, you may think? Perhaps, if you were limited by your own skills. By now I hope you've learned that's not the case. Instead, the pathway toward the blended family I have described is to reach out to Jesus Christ and ask Him to express these qualities of His life in your home. He indwells you, so each of these qualities resides in you at this moment. The key is to abandon your own self-efforts and yield yourself as a wife and mother to Him, asking Him to work through you. Talk to your family about the importance of this approach and model it until they see the beauty of the grace walk and find the Holy Spirit moving them in the same direction.

A blended family can be a greatly blessed family. Never allow yourself to think that God sees your marriage and family as His second-best for you because of the failure of your first marriage. God is able to show His goodness to the world through you, your husband, and your children. He loves to turn things that others underestimate into trophies of His grace.

Nothing and nobody that God builds comes in second place. He has always worked through broken things, small starts, despised things, weak people, people without reputation and status...things that seem unlikely to be divine vessels. He loves to touch them by His grace, lift them up, and show them to the world around. He speaks through these things, saying, "See how big and gracious I am. *This* is how I operate!" That is His pattern. You can see it repeated in the Bible again and again. So yield your blended family to Him and ask Him to glorify Himself in and through you. Then be ready because His grace is just that good.

19

Unscrambling Eggs

*L*ena's story causes any mother to cringe—especially moms with similar stories. Hers is all too common, but like every other person who has suffered, she is a prime candidate for receiving the restorative grace of God. Grace is the cure for every seemingly tragic situation. No circumstance is beyond redemption in the light of God's loving grace.

Lena and Scott married at 17 and 18, respectively. Lena was four months pregnant when they married. In September of that year, Barry was born. They had hoped his birth would bring stability to their already rocky marriage, but as parents often discover, nothing could have been further from reality.

Barry often cried much of the night. Lena's mother kept him during the day while Lena attempted to complete high school and Scott worked loading trucks for a shipping company, but the situation was difficult. With little sound sleep, the young parents found themselves becoming more and more agitated and short tempered with each other.

Marrying had seemed like a good idea when they first discovered Lena was pregnant, but before long they both began to question whether they had done the right thing by getting married. Barry was four now and full of energy. They both loved their child, but the problems between them intensified. As the conflict grew, bitterness built up between them. During one argument, Scott finally blurted out, "I don't think I can take this marriage anymore!" Lena agreed, and that was that. Sixty days later they were divorced.

Lena moved back into her parents' home. For a while everything seemed to be much smoother in life. In fact, it was almost like old times, before she had gotten pregnant or married. She went to school every day and then came home and helped care for Barry.

Unfortunately, the peaceful period didn't last long. As the months progressed and Lena became accustomed to the new living situation, she began to push the boundaries of her own behavior with her mother. Sometimes she hung out with her friends after school and didn't arrive home until close to five. Her mother didn't appreciate it and often said so.

Tension between Lena and her mother began to grow. Her mother had a set of expectations about Lena's behavior, and Lena's actions didn't fit those expectations. She told her mother, "I have a life too. At my age I can't stay locked down like a prisoner every day just because I have a child." Her mother explained to her that she wasn't a prisoner, but she did need to behave like a responsible parent.

As her senior year of college came to a close, Lena spent more and more time with a new boyfriend. Al knew she had a son, but when school ended and they both graduated, he asked her to move in with him. Lena's mother wasn't happy about the decision, but Lena took Barry and moved out anyway.

She and Al lived together for almost four years. One day, to her absolute surprise, Al came home from work and told her he was moving out. When she asked why, he didn't answer directly, but she began to realize that he had met somebody else. Al never admitted it, but Lena was convinced that was the reason behind his decision.

Unable to afford the apartment alone, she took her child and moved into a one-bedroom apartment near the restaurant where she worked as a server. Her work schedule was erratic there. Sometimes she worked days and at other times nights. Things were okay when she worked during the day because Barry was old enough to be in school by now. When she worked nights, Lena would asked her mother or a friend to watch him until she could leave work.

Over the years, Lena was absent from Barry's life much of the time. She partied with friends after work at night but told her mother she was working. The years clicked by until I met Lena. She was 34.

Shortly before I met Lena, a friend had shared the gospel with her, and she had begun to follow Christ. A big part of her motivation to become a believer was that Barry, who was now 17, was having disciplinary problems. He had been arrested for underage drinking once and for possession of marijuana twice. He was also talking about dropping out of school, a decision that Lena had learned the hard way was unwise.

"I know this is all my fault," Lena said to me one day. "If I had acted like a responsible adult instead of like an immature brat, things would be different. I've been a horrible mother, and now I'm paying for it. You can't go back and unscramble eggs."

What would you say to Lena? Her assessment that you can't unscramble eggs is true, isn't it? Some things seem impossible to undo regardless of how sorry we might be for our actions that caused them.

Maybe you can relate to Lena's sense of regret. Many women have given birth to babies before they were adults. Sometimes the child suffers the consequences of the mother's poor choices during that time of immaturity. Consequently, many mothers feel regret, guilt, shame, and an overall sense of failure as parents. What is the answer for those in that situation?

Grace in Our Messes

Grace doesn't appear like a magic fairy and rewrite the past. Rather, it steps into our difficult situations and begins its redemptive work. Remember that grace is actually a person named Jesus, and He not only involves Himself in our messy situations, He *rushes* in. The light of our Father's grace shows up brightest in the darkness of our lives. Where sin abounds, grace indeed does much more abound.

The first thing mothers like Lena need to do is to stop living in the past, suffocating under a smothering barrage of what-ifs and "If only I had…" Your life is what it is. Grace often doesn't erase the effects of our choices. If you live in either the past or the future, you'll slide deeper and deeper into despair.

Grace will begin to bring needed change as you focus on God's goodness. Look to Him and stop looking backward. He is the great I AM, and He is with you right now in the nitty-gritty details of your life to help you and your children in this present moment.

Don't live in regrets about the past. Don't live in fearful imaginary scenarios of the future. Live in the now. That's where God promises to be with you. Watch for Him to work in your child's life today. Then do the same thing again tomorrow. God *is* at work because He loves you and your children more than you could imagine.

Forgive Yourself

Forgiveness is the conscious decision to release somebody from anything we believe they owe us because of their offenses. What do you do when the one who has hurt you most is yourself? You forgive yourself.

Maybe you've beaten yourself up emotionally and mentally. You may live under a burden of blame that you manufacture by the ton. When we have failed, it is easy to become our own judge, jury, and executioner. We hear taunting voices in our own minds pointing out how we have failed, shaming us with reminders that we should have known better, and threatening us with imaginary scenarios of what could happen in the future because of the bad choices we've made.

There is only one way to get out from under that self-imposed curse. Praying about it is good, but praying alone won't solve it. Reading the Bible may bring temporary relief, but it won't completely cure the problem. All the religious activity you can crank out will only put a Band-Aid on the problem. The only thing that will free you from self-imposed guilt and shame is to forgive yourself.

Your Father has already forgiven you for everything you've ever done to fail your child. *Your sins are forgiven you!* That is the message of the gospel of grace revealed in Jesus Christ. Don't give authority to opposing voices that would have you believe you aren't forgiven, because you are.

Realizing that God doesn't hold your failures against you can enable and motivate you to forgive yourself. Will you hold yourself to a higher standard than He does? Nothing could be more ridiculous or harmful. He has forgiven you, so the only thing left is for you to accept His forgiveness and forgive yourself. The word "repent" denotes the idea of changing your mind. Could you possibly need to repent, to change your mind about this matter of forgiveness by acknowledging that God really has forgiven you and that you now need to forgive yourself?

Perhaps writing a declaration of forgiveness would be helpful. Consider the following example.

> I, [insert your name], acknowledge that I have failed in my parental responsibilities. I wish I had done things I didn't do, and I wish I had not done things I did. I regret those choices, but I cannot change them now. But I *can* receive my God's forgiveness for my sins of omission and commission. At this moment, I hereby accept His forgiveness for my shortcomings and my sins. Additionally, I forgive myself for those same things. I cannot change

the past or determine the future, but I will live in forgiveness in this moment. I will put the past behind me
and put the future in His hands. I will not live with
self-condemnation, guilt, or shame anymore. I will keep
my focus on my Father and will trust in His ability to
redeem my life and the life of my child. My hope is in
Him, and this is where I will stand.

Does this affirmation express the way you want to live your life?
If so, step forward in faith and make it your own declaration of
faith. Take the time to write it down on a separate piece of paper.
Then read it aloud so that your own words will validate your personal ownership of its content. Put the paper in a safe, handy place,
and anytime your thoughts or emotions tempt you to embrace guilt
and shame again, take out the paper and read it with faith and bold
affirmation.

My challenge to you is to accept your Father's forgiveness, forgive yourself, and then stand in the truth regardless of your feelings. Feelings don't normally change instantly, but as you continue
to stand in the truth of His forgiveness and of your own forgiveness,
your emotions will gradually conform to your consistent confession.
Do this and stand strong in it, and you'll be amazed by the healing
power you experience in the days to come.

Commit Your Child to the One Who Loves Him Most

It's easy to believe the lie that our failures always have permanent
and devastating effects on our children. That's simply not true. There
is always the possibility that grace will intervene. You may think that
scrambled eggs can't be unscrambled, but God can do anything.

For instance, you probably know that the wisest man in the Bible
is Solomon. Do you know the identity of his mother? She was Bathsheba, the one who committed adultery with David and whose husband was killed in the cover-up.

So by the time Solomon was born to David and Bathsheba,

they had committed adultery, arranged for Uriah to be killed, and watched the child of that affair die. Yet Solomon was a great king of Israel who had wealth, wisdom, and power. He built the first temple in Jerusalem. Thank God, His grace is bigger than our foolishness! Wrong choices don't have to follow you, punishing you for the rest of your life. Grace can put them to rest.

Don't assume your own failures will have ongoing negative effects in your child's life. God can step in anytime and change things completely. Some people with less than stellar backgrounds have made great contributions to the kingdom of God.

Commit your child into the hands of God and trust Him. Your ability to be involved in your child's development will largely depend on his age and openness to your input. Don't panic if your child doesn't respond to your guidance. Your Father is able to speak into his life in many ways. Trust Him to make His voice heard at the appropriate time and in the most effective way.

I met a mother a few years ago whose story touched me deeply. Her son was in prison, but she told me, "I am so thankful for him being there. God has transformed his life in prison. He radiates Christ now. He is happier there than I've ever seen him. He is touching the lives of many others around him in supernatural ways. God's hand is on my son."

No mother would wish for a testimony like hers, but it goes to show one important thing. God is in control and can bring light into the darkest situations of our lives or the lives of our children. Not every song is written in the major keys. However, some songs that are written in the minor keys, although mournful, are deeply moving and highly impactful.

Your God can arrange the individual notes of your child's life into a miraculous melody. If your child's life seems like a discordant, out-of-tune cacophony of confusion right now, just wait. In the end, the notes of all our lives will converge into a symphony that magnifies God's sovereignty and great grace.

Wherever you are, wherever your children are, this composition is not over yet. Look to the Great Composer and cling to the certainty that He abandons nobody. He never wipes His hands of our messy lives and walks away. He is here, with us for the duration. Our "no" has already been muted by the victorious shout of His eternal "yes!" He is committed to never stop loving us, never stop leading us, and never stop calling us to rest in His eternal embrace.

He is the Shepherd who leaves the ninety-nine to seek out the one. That one may be your son or daughter. You can rest. He came to seek and to save those who are lost, and nothing can deter Him from His divine mission.

Physical Abuse

Deena showed up at my office with a black eye and a downcast demeanor. I had been counseling her for about a month, and I knew that her husband had a serious problem controlling his anger. Deena and Spencer had come to the first two counseling sessions together, but then I asked him if he had considered the possibility that he had a problem with his temper.

"No!" he shouted. "No! I will not do this!"

"Will not do what?" I asked.

"I will not come to these sessions unless you address the real problem!"

"What do you think is the real problem?" I asked.

"Her!" he shouted.

That was the last time I had seen him. In our previous session, Deena had told me that Spencer had grabbed their eight-year-old by the shoulders and violently shaken him as he screamed at him. Deena had stood idly by but felt guilty for doing nothing.

"Can I assume that your black eye has something to do with all we've talked about?" I now asked her.

Tears began to flood her eyes.

"What happened?" I asked.

"He pinned me against the wall by my shoulders and head-butted me," she answered as she broke down and cried.

According to the National Library of Medicine, domestic violence is the most common cause of injury to women ages 15 to 44.* Sadly, many of those women will suffer in silence, mistakenly believing their situation is rare. Physical violence is one of the most demeaning experiences a wife can know. This marriage conflict must take priority in being resolved because it tends to escalate and can quickly become very dangerous.

There is no room for physical abuse in your marriage—none. Deena described how it began with Spencer while they were still dating. One day she was eating peanuts and cracking the shells with her teeth. "Stop it," Spencer said.

"It's just peanuts," Deena answered as she continued to crack the shells.

"Stop cracking those shells with your teeth. It's driving me crazy," he replied.

Deena continued, and soon Spencer reached across the car seat and slapped her hand, sending the peanuts flying everywhere. "I told you to *stop it!*" he yelled.

Deena's eyes filled with tears, but she didn't say anything. After that, nothing more was mentioned about the incident. She told herself that Spencer had been under a lot of stress lately and that he had, after all, asked her to stop. She did what many physically abused women do—she took partial blame for the incident.

Indicators like this should never be taken casually. Diminishing the seriousness of what Spencer had done was the doorway that would lead Deena into a world of abuse she had never imagined. She made the tragic mistake of believing that there is such a thing as a *minor* incident of physical violence. Had she seen the seriousness of Spencer's behavior, she could have responded appropriately, and things may have turned out very differently for her.

---

* http://answers.usa.gov/system/selfservice.controller?configuration=1000&partition_id=1
&cmd=view_article&article_id=11241&usertype=1&language=en&country=us

Before speaking about wives who are physically abused, a word about the potential for ministry in this area may be helpful. You may be able to help keep single women from the kind of horror Deena has known by reminding them that physical abuse should never be tolerated. When you encourage your daughter, another family member, or a friend to have no tolerance for the slightest expression of physical violence, you express love to her.

When a man violently jerks something out of a woman's hand, that action should be a major red flag for reassessing the relationship. That sort of behavior clearly shows that the man has little control over his impulses. Shaking, squeezing a woman's hand or arm with intention of hurting, angrily grabbing her by the shoulders, or even causing pain and then suggesting he was just playing is not acceptable. This sort of behavior is a five-bell alarm that every woman needs to recognize. As noted when the matter of bullying was discussed in an earlier chapter, a man may ask, "Can't you take a joke?" But those men must be plainly and forcefully told that hurting somebody is not a joke and will not be tolerated for an instant.

Any single woman would be well advised to never marry a man who may be prone to violent behavior. Many women make excuses and turn a blind eye to these warnings to their own detriment. When it comes to marrying, physical abuse is a deal-breaker, plain and simple.

Now let's consider those who are already married to abusive men. What is a wife to do if her husband is physically abusive? To answer that question, let's consider what needs to take place with her internally and then externally. In other words, some things must happen in her mind, and then other things must follow in her actions.

Internal Liberation

This book has stated from the beginning that the solution to any problem we face is the grace of God expressed through Jesus Christ. Does God expect a wife to subject herself to abusive behavior from her husband? Absolutely not. As discussed in chapter 8,

"Confronting Bullies," to allow your husband's abusive behavior to go unchallenged is not only dangerous for you but also a great disservice to him. It communicates that such behavior is acceptable—but *it is not!*

Grace can empower and motivate us to forsake passivity and become proactive about our situation. Does loving your husband require you to sacrifice yourself on the altar of his misbehavior? Does being a good wife mean you just accept whatever comes? To answer those questions, consider what Jesus said about loving other people. He said to "love your neighbor as yourself" (Mark 12:31).

You absolutely must have a healthy respect for yourself if you are to relate in a loving and healthy way toward others, including your husband. Would you allow anybody else you love—your daughter, your mother, your sister, your friend—to be physically abused? Would you be passive in that situation? Of course you wouldn't. If you saw anybody else you love being abused, you would rightfully step up to help her. That's what love does.

Jesus said we are to love others as we love ourselves. Does it seem wrong to love yourself? It shouldn't, because that's the baseline Jesus gave for understanding how to love other people. I'm not talking about an egotistical narcissism. Rather, I'm referring to a genuine and appropriate self-respect. Without a healthy, loving respect for our own dignity, we are ill equipped to relate to others in a healthy way.

Most abused wives' opinion of themselves has spiraled downward. They deplore the mistreatment they receive, but many hear an underlying voice deep within them that lies to them, telling them that they deserve it. The lies cause them to feel complicit in the whole situation, as if they are somehow partially to blame for what's going on. You must be set free from these thoughts and feelings in order to make the necessary external steps.

Read the following words carefully: *You do not deserve to be abused.* Read those words again and this time, pray that the Holy

Spirit will plant the truth of the statement deep in your mind, your emotions, and your will.

An internal healing must take place in you before you are able to take the external actions necessary to change the situation. Healing always comes from the inside out, not the other way around. The first step in your healing is for the Spirit of Jesus, who lives inside you, to establish within you the truth of who you are. You are...

a member of the bride of Christ (2 Corinthians 11:2)

a divine work of art (Ephesians 2:10)

His beloved (Romans 9:25)

precious to Him (Isaiah 43:4)

a child of God (Galatians 3:26)

a person of great value (Matthew 6:26-30)

That's just the beginning of the list. You must learn this reality if you are to be healthy and develop healthy relationships to others.

Apart from the love of Christ, people generally will not respect you more than you respect yourself. A lack of self-respect always comes from a lack of self-esteem. Don't be mistaken about what I'm saying. I am not suggesting that you just need good self-esteem. It's not simply a matter of feeling better about yourself. What you need is a *godly* self-esteem. Your perception of yourself needs to be based on who God says you truly are.

My goal isn't to try to pump you up emotionally or make you feel better. My intention isn't simply to make you think positive thoughts about yourself. My desire is for you to see yourself the way your Creator sees you. *That* will be the catalyst of your healing.

I cannot overstate the importance of seeing yourself through God's eyes. Wives who have been abused have heard negative messages about themselves throughout their lives. Those lying messages undermine the truth about your true worth. They must be obliterated by the grace of God and be replaced with the truth about your real identity.

As long as you feel, think, and act as if abuse were acceptable, the situation is not likely to change. As you grow in God-given confidence of your true value, you will become equipped to take outward steps to change the situation.

Rise Up in Grace

Grace provides the divine enablement for us to be all that God has created us to be and to do all that He has called us to do. Sometimes wives who have been abused believe they can avoid further conflict by managing the situation so their husbands don't become angry. They discover their husbands' emotional triggers by trial and error and try to avoid them.

Despite the wives' best efforts, many husbands still find reasons to become angry and abusive. An emotionally and physically battered wife files away those new reasons and tries to add those behaviors to the list of actions she must avoid. This is like the life of a prisoner under a cruel tyrant, and your God does not intend for you to live that way. You must believe that.

What are you to do? Become proactive about facilitating a change in your relationship that stops this sort of behavior. Many wives believe it's easier *not* to proactively facilitate change. Understandably, they are afraid that any attempt to stop the bad behavior will only make matters worse. As difficult as it is for them, these wives have learned to walk on eggshells in order not to upset their husbands, and they have convinced themselves that for the most part, it is working out fairly well. They are believing their own lie.

If you are being abused, it is time for the abuse to stop. Now. The first step is to appropriate the grace of Jesus Christ within you. That will empower you to rise up and do whatever is necessary to see the change come. Your heavenly Father loves you dearly and most certainly will guide your thoughts and decisions about how to move forward to correct a wrong that should never have happened. Don't condemn yourself about what has happened. Be zealous in taking the necessary actions so you can experience that which God intends for you.

Seek Out Support

So then, a wife who has been abused must become assertive and seek change. This is an admirable step because it requires great courage and faith. You are not likely to be able to complete this process alone. You need emotional and sometimes even practical, logistical support to follow through with your decision to stop the abuse.

It is important that once you decide to stop the abuse, you follow through with your decision. If you abandon your pursuit for change when you encounter opposition from your husband, you may make matters worse. So remember and appropriate the biblical promises of Christ's support as you act in faith to facilitate change in your marriage. Your Father's desire is for you to live free of abuse for the rest of your life.

Find a friend or two with whom you can be completely honest about your situation. These should be people with whom you have an intimate friendship already. Even if you feel embarrassed in sharing the truth with them, do it. Isolation is an enemy in situations of physical abuse. Too many abused wives are more concerned about what others will think of their husbands if they knew the truth than they are about their own safety and future. Give your husband's reputation to God and act in faith. You need help right now, and Jesus stands ready to offer it through these friends.

These will be people you can call in an emergency. They will be your emotional support and will be there for you should you need to suddenly leave your home for your own safety. They should be able to provide a safe place or help you find one. These friends will be lifelines who are willing to be there for you on a moment's notice.

You would be also wise to locate helpful professional resources in your area. Most communities have agencies or organizations that are available to help battered women. Don't be too proud to call on them. You can call the National Domestic Violence Hotline at 1-800-799-7233 (SAFE) in the United States or 1-800-363-9010 in Canada. In the United Kingdom, call Women's Aid at 0808 2000 247. Australian wives can call 1-800-737-7328 (RESPECT). If you live in other parts of the world, visit the International Directory of Domestic Violence Agencies online (www.hotpeachpages.net) for a global list of help lines, shelters, and crisis centers. Finally, if you are in immediate danger, dial 911 (or 999 in some countries) and have the police come immediately. You must protect yourself and your children at all costs.

Discuss the Problem with Your Husband

It is important that you have a discussion with your husband and tell him in no uncertain terms that you will no longer allow yourself to be abused. Explain in a calm but confident way that you will take whatever steps are necessary to protect yourself and that you will no longer tolerate certain actions. Your emotions will most likely be fragile as you have this conversation, but speak in a bold and matter-of-fact way that communicates your resolve to him.

How you respond to acts of abuse will depend on the situation. If he jerks something out of your hand in anger, that calls for a response. Slapping your face would call for a different response. The point is that you must know what you're going to do. Determine in advance how you're going to respond so you won't have to decide in the heat of the moment. Then follow through.

You cannot allow your husband to think you are bluffing. You must do whatever is necessary to ensure that he begins to respect you. If you have to call the police, do it. If you need to leave your house, do it. Your decisive action may convince your husband that you are serious about this matter.

It is important for your husband to meet with a counselor. The counselor will probably want to talk to you both together first. Then, once your husband's anger issue is identified, the counselor may want to meet with him alone. Explain to your husband that it is important to you that he demonstrate his love for you by receiving counseling. Make sure again that he knows you will no longer accept the mistreatment you have tolerated in the past.

Leaving Your Husband

I suggested to Deena that she consider leaving Spencer because he was unwilling to change. I explained that a separation might bring him to his senses so he could see the seriousness of the matter. When people misbehave, sometimes they need someone to shake them up—or wake them up!

I spoke to Deena about her primary responsibility to her children and their physical welfare. I reminded her that when Spencer kicked them, shook them, slapped them, and so on, she was complicit in his crime if she continued to allow it. Physical abuse isn't simply a relationship problem. It is a crime, punishable by law. Women and children *must* be protected. There is no excuse for failure in this area.

At first, Deena was concerned about how a separation would affect their lives. Her husband was a staff member of their local church. She knew that his reputation would be ruined and that he could lose his position. I walked through the possibilities with her, and she realized that even the worst scenario was better than a lifetime of abuse.

Remember that when a person is broken, he often comes to see his fleshly actions and his need to turn to God in repentance and faith. Pain can be a valuable tool in our Father's hands. I'm not suggesting that you try to hurt your husband, but it's not your job to protect him either. Do you understand and believe that? You need to do what is best for you and your children and then leave your husband's predicament in God's hands. He will use it for your husband's good.

If you need to leave, leave. One thing is certain—it is not your

Father's will for you to be physically hurt. Don't put this issue up for a vote among all your friends. Unless they have lived with abuse, they cannot understand your situation and lack the experience they would need to advise you.

You can be assured that you are a precious possession of your heavenly Father. He does not intend for you to allow yourself to be abused. Trust Him and then do whatever you need to do to respect and love yourself the way your Father respects and loves you. It will probably be scary, but when you trust Him and act in faith, He will guide you each step of the way.

Emotional Absence

Sometimes I feel like I'm living with a zombie!" Sherri said. "What makes a man act like this? I think he's totally oblivious to what I think and feel."

Sherri and Troy have been married almost 34 years. Some would say Troy isn't a talker, but Sherri doesn't see it that way. "He doesn't have any trouble talking when he wants something from me, especially sex. I can always tell what's on his mind when he turns on his Mr. Outgoing personality, but other than that I can hardly get a word out of him."

This situation isn't new to Troy and Sherri, but it has worsened over the years. Sherri has sometimes thought things might change, but they haven't. "Just when I think we've really taken a step forward, he does something that shows he never understood a thing I said. What does it take to get through to him?"

Wives whose husbands are withdrawn and seldom communicative have good reason to be frustrated. If a marriage is to be anything, it is to be an interactive relationship. A wife needs her husband to nurture a strong, loving relationship, and when that doesn't happen, it is normal for her to feel frustration, disappointment, and even anger. It's not easy when the person you love seems to have gone into emotional hibernation. The question is, is there hope for a man like this? Will he *ever* change, or must a wife resign herself to a one-sided relationship?

What's the Problem?

If your husband is emotionally distant despite your best efforts to help him to engage with you, don't automatically assume that he doesn't feel emotions. That is seldom the case. In counseling, these men typically report that they do feel emotion but that they just don't express their feelings the way their wives want them to. "Some things go without saying," Troy told Sherri one time when she was pressing the issue with him.

Some men project an emotional unavailability because that is what they have learned. Their own fathers may have modeled this. Men who grew up in homes where their fathers showed little emotion and acted as stern, no-nonsense disciplinarians don't have a foundation for any other behavior. A strict authoritarian father who withholds tender emotions and fails to engage with his wife and family in casual and warm conversation often unwittingly sets his own son on the pathway toward the same kind of behavior. That isn't to say a husband can't learn to behave differently, but it does give a reason why he may act as he does. A wife can take some comfort in the fact that his actions really aren't intended to be an insult to her, nor do they mean he doesn't care.

A husband may also seem emotionally absent if he has been hurt in the past and now guards his emotions to protect himself. Emotional withdrawal in marriage is a flesh pattern, an independent coping mechanism that one uses to minimize the likelihood of feeling rejection. It is independent in the sense that the husband isn't yielding that area of his life to Christ, but is trying to handle it himself.

Open expressions of love are always somewhat risky. Even the life of Jesus demonstrates that fact. The apostle John writes that Jesus came to His own, but His own did not receive Him. Jesus surely knew He would be rejected by His own people, but because of love He gave Himself completely anyway. He produces that kind of behavior when He lives through husbands today.

A healthy expression of love risks disappointment and rejection. Many emotionally absent husbands have not yielded their emotions to Christ, but seek to manage their feelings themselves instead. Insecurity can cause a man to guard himself in this distorted and unhealthy way.

In addition, men generally don't process life exactly like women do. In particular, they are often less likely to want to talk about sensitive subjects. For many men, lengthy discussions of some subjects simply aren't necessary. They would rather make a short assessment of the overall situation, find what they believe to be a quick solution, and close the book on the matter. Their wives are often inclined to be verbal processors who talk through a subject until a resolution is found. Men who act emotionally absent are not at all comfortable with that approach.

Sherri pictured this aspect well one day when she said, "I pour my heart out to him and he responds with a grunt." When she pressed the matter with Troy, he finally answered, "I thought we'd already discussed this." To her, a discussion includes two people sharing their feelings and thoughts. To Troy, the discussion happened when she talked and he offered a solution in a succinct few words. He couldn't understand why Sherri wanted to come back to the same subject and rehash it. It was already settled to him, but they had barely scratched the surface as far as Sherri was concerned.

Dead-End Approaches

Sometimes a wife whose husband is emotionally aloof will try to pressure him into talking about his feelings. Many have learned the hard way that this approach seldom works. Instead of talking, a husband may explain that he doesn't know what she wants him to say, and then he will simply shut down. If she continues to pressure him to talk, she will only put more distance between them. Don't try to force your husband to share his feelings. It won't work and usually does more harm than good.

Another dead-end approach is to make comparisons. Sherri made the mistake one day of comparing her relationship with Troy to another couple. "Stan and Lori talk all the time," she said. "Lori told me they almost always lie in bed and talk at night before they go to sleep."

An approach like that is a sure way to tighten the emotional vise on a husband. Whatever causes him to be closed certainly will never be relaxed by making a comparison. The only thing he hears is that he doesn't measure up to another woman's husband. Never compare your husband to another man. It can do inestimable damage to any possibility of seeing him open up and begin to talk.

A third approach that won't work is to use emotional leverage to open him up. Many wives will complain or even cry, expressing that they don't feel loved. These expressions may be sincere. Wives may be understandably disillusioned about not feeling emotionally valued. They may have every right to complain, to cry, to scold, or to rant, but the outcome must be considered in advance. Here are some of the ways most emotionally absent husbands will react.

He may maintain the silent treatment. Troy seemed to simply tune out when Sherri tried to pressure him into an in-depth discussion of the problem. She simply couldn't get a conversation out of him. "Do you even care?" she asked.

"Of course I care," he calmly replied.

"Then talk to me," she responded.

"I don't know what you want me to say."

Of course, this kind of response can be maddening to a wife, but it's very common in situations like this. You may not like hearing your husband respond that way, but you're certainly not alone.

Or a husband may humor his wife. Sometimes, in an attempt to bring closure to the matter, a husband will say whatever he thinks his wife wants to hear. His goal is to keep her from rocking the boat, so he will say whatever he believes will calm the tempest. He has no intentions of actually doing anything different. He simply wants the current conversation to end.

Emotionally absent husbands use many other responses when confronted about not keeping up their commitment to communicate. They may agree to change but procrastinate, become overly engaged in sports or other leisure activities, begin to work more hours, or lose their temper.

Identifying Unresolved Conflicts

The situation described thus far in this chapter may sound bleak, but I want you to see that you aren't alone. If you recognize your own marriage in what has been said already, at least you can take heart in knowing that there are others in a similar situation. Yours is not an isolated experience. That alone can bring some encouragement.

My goal isn't to vilify husbands who behave this way either. People are the way they are for various reasons. Something has caused your husband to be emotionally withdrawn. It's very unlikely that one day he made a conscious decision to simply shut down emotionally and that he has been committed to that decision since then.

One area to explore is related to unresolved conflict in your marriage. Was there a time when your husband wasn't emotionally absent? Did his behavior suddenly change? If so, what precipitated that change? Ask the Holy Spirit to show you and your husband whether a specific incident caused him to develop a habit of withdrawal.

If he hasn't always been withdrawn, something happened. People don't suddenly and radically change for no reason. Talk to him about it and ask him if he knows the cause. If he agrees that he hasn't always been this way but doesn't know why he changed, ask him to pray with you, and ask your Father to show you the cause. Remember that withdrawal is often a defense mechanism to protect oneself from hurt. Consider that possibility as you pray together.

If your husband has always been emotionally absent to you, think back to the beginning of your relationship. Did you believe you could change him? Did you think that after you were married, he would behave differently? What was it about your husband that caused you to love him even though he was withdrawn? Look for the things you appreciated then and focus on them now. This won't necessarily make your frustration disappear, but it will at least help you focus on the qualities that attracted you to him.

If your husband was withdrawn from the time you met him, perhaps a childhood incident of conflict or rejection led to the sort of coping approach you see in him now. Ask him about that possibility and pray together about it. Time doesn't necessarily heal all wounds. Sometimes the infections from wounds become worse over time. Perhaps your husband has some old emotional wounds that need divine healing.

True Communication

If you have an emotionally absent husband, the most important consideration is whether you and he communicate clearly. He may resist communication, suggesting that everything is fine.

It is important for your husband to understand that even though things may be fine to him, you often feel as if he doesn't value you or love you. When you talk to him about your feelings, describe the way you feel. Try not to sound as if you're accusing him, or he will naturally feel attacked and become defensive.

Your initial goal isn't for him to admit any guilt, but simply for him to understand you. That's the first step. No change is possible until you both understand what the other is thinking and feeling.

Don't expect your husband to pour out his thoughts on the

subject. You know better than that. However, you can ask him to respond to you in a way that shows that he has listened and understood what you are saying. Don't give a long speech about the subject. Briefly and simply describe how you feel. You might say, "I feel…" and then use feeling words, such as "unloved," "unappreciated," or "rejected." Don't say, "I feel like you don't care." That's not a feeling, it's an opinion—almost an accusation. At this point you want him to recognize your *feelings*, so focus specifically on that. Your goal at this point isn't to change his behavior, but to be heard and understood. You'll be amazed how much that step alone will help you.

If your husband discounts your feelings, suggesting that you shouldn't feel that way or that he doesn't know why you would feel that way, don't become defensive. Instead, say something like, "Well, whether I should feel that way or not, it *is* how I feel. I need you to help me with this. I love you, and for you to work with me on this is one of the best ways I can think of for you to love me right now. Will you help me?"

After you have described your feelings to him, ask for feedback. You might say, "What did you hear me say? I want to be sure I'm being clear." Don't suggest that you want to be sure he understands. You want to focus not on his ability to understand, but on your ability to be clear. That can help prevent him from feeling defensive.

If he says he understands, don't accept that generic statement. Ask him to tell you what he heard you say so you'll know you're on the same wavelength. He needs to restate what you've said in different words. If his response shows he has missed something, fill in the blanks and ask him again to tell you what he has heard.

These basic listening skills, developed by Drs. Dallas and Nancy Demmitt, can help you tremendously. Feeling that your husband has truly heard you and knowing that you have been understood are important first steps toward a successful resolution.

Does He Want to Change?

The cornerstone of the whole matter is, does he want to change? He may suggest that things seem fine to him. Husbands who are emotionally unavailable to their wives commonly feel that way. If your husband is willing to participate in the kind of discussion and feedback explained in the section above, you can be very encouraged. Affirm him for participating in this first step. Assure him that this path will lead to a mutually satisfying resolution to the situation. Bring this first step to a positive conclusion so that he will be more likely to engage the next time you want to continue.

You may discover that your husband is simply not willing to discuss the matter at all. He might not be interested in taking any steps to change anything at the moment. Remember, if you believe this is the case with your husband, it is important to have him verify by his words that he isn't interested in the sort of exchange we have described.

If your husband is reluctant, that doesn't necessarily mean he doesn't care. He could be uncomfortable about the expectations that could be placed on him if he agrees. He may be tentative about the unknown. Assure your husband that you aren't going to ask him to do anything except let you know that he understands what you tell him. "I just want to explain how I'm feeling. I need to say some things and know I've been understood. That's all. Will you help me with that?"

The limitations of space here won't allow a detailed step-by-step description of how to proceed with this process. Generally speaking, it may be helpful to have several discussions like the one suggested in the preceding paragraphs. This will allow you to be heard and understood and will also show your husband that you aren't going to accuse, interrogate, or prosecute him. As he feels more comfortable and realizes that these conversations are nonthreatening, you will recognize a time when it is appropriate to ask him what he thinks and feels about your relationship.

Open and heartfelt dialogue commonly leads to gradual healing. Be patient. Don't become upset by apparent setbacks. This kind of growth isn't a constant incline upward, but as long as you are generally moving forward, you are in a good place.

Couples commonly reach a place where they recognize that counseling may be helpful. If you find yourselves at that place, don't hesitate to ask for help. Objective, outside parties who are skilled at discussing situations like yours have been a great help to many couples.

If it becomes clear that your husband simply isn't going to take even the first step of talking with you, there is no need in trying to force it. You will understandably feel hurt, but don't allow yourself to emotionally explode on him. It would be better to leave the room and wait until you can *respond* to him calmly instead of *reacting* with raw and volatile emotions.

The Long, Quiet Road

Sometimes there is no change despite all that a wife has done to facilitate progress with an emotionally absent husband. Maybe you've already said and done all the things I've suggested. Perhaps you hoped this chapter would provide the secret to the change you've longed to see in your husband, but you haven't found the answer you hoped to find.

There is no magic formula to apply to your situation. You can't force your husband to change. What can you do? The better question to ask is, what can you *know*? If something were left for you to do, you would have done it by now. But our loving Father doesn't abandon wives in this painful situation. When nothing seems to be left for you to do, you still have one more option. Trust Him. His presence in your life can teach you some things that will sustain you.

Your God Is with You

In no way would I seek to minimize your painful feelings if your husband is emotionally absent. Rather, I want to remind you that you are deeply loved by your Creator. Regardless of whether you ever hear your husband say or show it, *you are precious.*

Refuse to believe that your husband is emotionally ignoring you because something is inherently wrong with you. The problem is not within you. You have been created as a divine masterpiece and are deeply loved by Jesus Christ. He will never leave you or forsake you.

Although your circumstances may be sad, they can lead you to experience and revel in the love of God more than you ever have—perhaps more than you ever would have if your circumstances were different. Ask Him to reveal His love to you. This may sound hollow right now, but it is completely true: No person is intended to meet the deepest needs of another person. Our God designed us in such a way that only He can do that.

Learn to lean into His love and discover your identity in Him. See yourself as one who loves you in a greater way than anyone else could. Allow your relationship with Him to define you because He is the true source of your authentic value.

God Isn't Finished with Your Husband

Don't give up hope. Your God is a God of miracles. I have seen men change in an instant when God's hand reaches into their lives and touches them. He can do the same for your husband.

Why hasn't He done it already? Only He knows the answer to that question. We could ask the same question of a multitude of things. Why hasn't He brought world peace? Why hasn't He ended poverty, war, crime, and hatred? Some questions must be laid squarely in the lap of Mystery with the knowledge that His thoughts are far above ours and that He acts in ways that fit His plans and timing, not ours.

Don't allow yourself to become bitter. Keep your eyes on Jesus Christ and know that He hasn't forgotten your need or your prayers. Cling to Jesus. When you feel emotionally lonely, cling to Him.

When you feel rejected, cling to Him. When you feel nobody cares, cling to Him. Cling to Jesus. He loves you deeply and dearly. He holds you in His tender embrace at this moment and assures you, "You are so precious to me. I love you *so* much." Cling to Jesus and know this: He will forever cling to you.

Unfailing Love

I wrote this book to encourage you as a wife and a mother. My goal has been to direct your attention to Jesus Christ amid the stress and strain of walking out your faith so that you might come to rest in His gracious empowerment. He wants you to enjoy the rest He promises and not become burned out by the demands you face every day.

Study the life of Jesus in the Gospels, and you'll learn that He didn't always yield to others' demands. When Mary and Martha sent word that their brother, Lazarus, was dying, Jesus didn't rush there. In fact, John 11 records that He waited three more days before going to their home. Martha wasn't happy about that decision at all, but Jesus understood something Martha didn't know at the time. Things always work out better when we trust our Father's schedule and simply do what He has put before us to do. Jesus did eventually arrive in Bethany, and He raised Lazarus from the dead.

Wives who walk in grace have found their pace, or to be more exact, they have found God's pace for them. Our homes are the most effective crucibles for testing our faith. Marriage and children will test the strength of our faith more than anything else in life. If there's a weak place in the wall, it will be discovered there.

Some chapters in this book may not have applied to you. But I suspect that when you read them, the Holy Spirit brought to your mind somebody whose life they could address. Perhaps in the days ahead He will allow you to share some of these truths with that person in a gracious and loving way.

This book has addressed women whose husbands are unbelievers, women whose husbands believe but are disinterested in spiritual things, and women whose husbands want to pressure their wives into sin, bullying, verbal abuse, and other challenging marital situations. We've discussed parenting, we've dealt with prodigals, and we've tried to find balance in blended families. In other words, the range of topics has been broad, but there is one thing I hope you will take away from this book.

It isn't within your own ability to change your husband or your children. I hope you see at this point that none of us can even change ourselves! Building a strong marriage and rearing children requires supernatural guidance. Neither is an exact science, and there are no definitive rules guaranteeing the perfect outcome we hope for in our marriage or children. You have learned many practical guidelines, but it is important to remember that unless those actions are animated by the life of Christ within you, they are nothing more than manipulative techniques that have no power to change anybody.

God's First Act and First Word to Couples

At the core of it all, the secret to a strong family life is surrender to the One who established the family in the beginning. When God created Adam and Eve, He didn't immediately give them a list of rules. Genesis 1:27-28 records the first moments after He created them.

> God created man in His own image, in the image of God
> He created him; male and female He created them.
> God blessed them; and God said to them, "Be fruitful
> and multiply, and fill the earth, and subdue it; and rule

over the fish of the sea and over the birds of the sky and
over every living thing that moves on the earth."

The first thing God did after creating Adam and Eve was to show
them His love. Notice the first act of God toward the first couple:
"God blessed them." Note the first words He spoke to them: "Be
fruitful and multiply." That action and those words reveal the heart
of your Father. He wants to bless you and wants you to be fruitful
in your marriage, your home, and your life in general.

The struggles of life sometimes blind us to God's ongoing intention toward us. But His purpose and plan for you, His faithfulness
and never-ending love for you, can fill you with optimism. As you
finish reading this book, take that optimism into your marriage
and your child rearing. Face each day with the confidence that He
is working in your life and in the lives of your family to fulfill the
plan He has had for you from the beginning.

Don't allow apparent roadblocks in your home to discourage
you. Don't lose hope that your Father is working in your life and the
lives of your husband and children. He is constantly at work, even
when you feel abandoned. Your God wants to bless you in your marriage, and He wants your family to be fruitful beyond your wild-
est dreams.

As I was writing this book, some wives asked me, "So are you
going to write another book for men, telling them how to walk in
grace with their wives?" I may indeed do that, but don't make the
mistake of believing that if your husband would change, your marriage would become all that you want it to be. Christ's life expressed
through you may be the key to the transformation you desire.

On the other hand, as you employ the concepts in this book,
God may use you to help your husband learn. Speaking the right
words in the right way at the right time can certainly lead to a right
result when the Holy Spirit is involved. Keep your eyes and ears
open for such opportunities.

Perhaps you have a strong marriage and read this book to be

encouraged in your own grace walk. I hope you have found helpful information here about Jesus Christ living through you in your relationship to your husband. As you have seen, most chapters have addressed specific things you can say or do. That's because walking in grace isn't a passive lifestyle. I wrote in the first chapter that the key to a successful relationship isn't what we do, but rather the person of Jesus Christ. However, that doesn't mean that there is never anything to do. It isn't legalistic to move toward a solution for problems or strengthen your marriage relationship.

Some have mistakenly believed that grace means we don't have to do anything, and they feel we shouldn't even discuss the *doing* aspect of our grace walk. But grace doesn't make us just sit and wait as if we were in a prison. God's grace often empowers us to rise up and act in the strength of His Spirit. You can take practical steps and move forward without being legalistic.

As I've implied numerous times in this book, the way to tell whether an action is legalistic is to determine its source. What gives life to an action? Is what we are doing an expression of the life of Christ through us, or is it our own independent attempt to manipulate the situation into what we want it to be? Are our actions expressing His life, or are we acting in our own power?

The answer isn't hard to identify. As you try some of the specific actions outlined in this book, ask yourself, "Am I trying to manipulate my husband, or am I acting in faith that this is what my Father wants me to do?" If you ask that question with an open heart and mind, the Holy Spirit within you will show you the answer. Trust Him to speak to you inwardly and to show you your true motives.

Here's one way you can know whether you're trying to make things happen yourself. Do you need to be in control of the outcome? Your role is to commit your marriage relationship to God, act in faith by saying and doing the things that you know are appropriate, and then leaving the results to Him.

God's character is revealed in His triune nature. He exists in three persons—Father, Son, and Holy Spirit. Community and communion are parts of His nature, so He has created us for these as well. The communion you share with your husband is a picture of the relationship that exists among the members of the Trinity and the church of Jesus Christ.

The apostle Paul wrote, "'For this reason a man shall leave his father and mother and shall be joined to his wife, and the two shall become one flesh.' This mystery is great; but I am speaking with reference to Christ and the church" (Ephesians 5:31-32).

In simple language, Paul explained that the union that exists between a husband and wife is a sacred picture of the oneness that Jesus Christ shares with His church. Your marriage is intended to show the world what divine union looks like. It is a visible relationship designed to proclaim what agape looks like in the invisible relationship between the church and its Head.

The final word I hope you will remember as you end this book is a word of grace. You probably picked up the book hoping that you would learn how to live as the wife and mother that your Father wants you to be. You may have hoped to discover helpful, biblical principles to incorporate into your relationship with your husband.

I hope that as you finish *When Wives Walk in Grace*, you will appropriate the reality that Jesus Christ is the builder of marriages. He is the source of any effective actions that strengthen our relationships. His grace is sufficient to transform you, your husband, and your home.

As you wait on Him and watch Him working in your marriage, it is important to function from a place of grace. Show grace to your husband when he fails. Understand that God's Spirit is working in him even when the progress is too slow to recognize. Celebrate the progress you see by acknowledging that you are witnessing nothing less than God at work.

Show yourself grace as well. That's so important. Too many sermons and books about being a godly wife leave women feeling as if they don't measure up, as if they need to try harder. That's not true. You are possessed by Agape, and He is giving you the knowledge and skills you need to be the wife He has called you to be.

When you fail, accept the fact that you aren't perfect and move on. Focus on your progress, not the pitfalls you will encounter along the way. You may need to entrust yourself, your husband, and your marriage into your Father's hands again and again. That's okay. Growth can't be charted with a steady incline of progress—it includes stops and starts. That's okay too because God won't give up on you regardless of how many setbacks you may seem to have. The One who has begun a good work in you really will complete it.

Self-effort will fail. Marriage techniques will fail. Determination will fail. But Love never fails (1 Corinthians 13:8). God has committed Himself to you and to your marriage, and He will not give up on you. So don't give up on Him or on the hope of an improved marriage. The One who set the first marriage in place will align yours with His purposes for you. Trust Him and wait for Him to bring it to pass.

A Personal Word

If reading *When Wives Walk in Grace* has helped you, I would be happy to hear from you. Authors are always encouraged when they receive feedback from those who have read their books. You may write to me at

Dr. Steve McVey
Grace Walk Ministries
PO Box 6537
Douglasville, GA 30135

You may also e-mail me at info@gracewalk.org. Visit our ministry website at www.gracewalk.org, where you can learn more about our ministry around the world. Every week, on our home page I post the "Sunday Preaching Program," a 30-minute teaching from the Bible that helps you live each day in the loving grace of your Father. The teachings are free and are always practical to daily living.

You can also connect with me through Facebook or through my blog at www.stevemcvey.com. My goal on these sites is to connect with readers at a more personal level.

I have written numerous other books in addition to this one, including the bestselling *Grace Walk*. They are available at gracewalk.org, as are a wide variety of CDs and DVD teachings I have produced. I invite you to visit our online store to browse many other writings and recordings that can help you in your own daily grace walk.

Finally, if *When Wives Walk in Grace* has encouraged you, will you share it with others? Many of us who believe that this message of grace needs to spread are working together to make it known to others. How can you help?

If you purchase a copy of this book through my office as a gift for somebody else, I will be happy to autograph it. Another way to help bring visibility to the book is to post positive reviews on online at sites that sell the book, such as Amazon.com.

Together we can reach out to encourage people with the transforming power of the gospel of grace. Self-effort and magic formulas cannot transform marriages. The living presence of Jesus Christ makes all the difference in a relationship. Join me in making this message known and then stay in contact with me to let me know what our Father is doing through you to reach others with the wonderful news of His transforming love!

Discussion Questions

Chapter 1: Kissing Frogs

1. In this chapter, what misunderstanding about marriage is illustrated by Russell Stover Candies, dieting, and frog princes?

2. In what ways do wives often attempt to change their husbands?

3. How does grace apply to a wife's desire to see her husband become the man God intends him to be?

4. List three differences between grace and self-help.

Chapter 2: Solo Spirituality

1. What are a few expectations that Christian wives commonly place on their husbands?

2. What can you do to cause your husband to assume his responsibilities as a Christian husband and father?

3. Describe the "push in–step back" principle. How does it relate to your attempt to get your husband to grow spiritually?

4. What are some differences between a religious family and a spiritual family?

Chapter 3: Second Thoughts

1. When a wife begins to wonder if she married the right man, what should she focus on instead? Why does that matter?

2. Name some Bible characters who made bad choices that God eventually redeemed and turned into something very good. How

might those examples help a wife who believes she married the wrong man because he wasn't a believer?

3. How is a wife to behave in a relationship with a man she knows is not a follower of Jesus Christ? In what ways can she influence him? In what ways does she need to avoid trying to influence him?

4. How does the doctrine of God's sovereignty relate to your concern about marrying the wrong man?

Chapter 4: Intrinsic Value

1. What is the danger of looking to your husband to validate your personal worth? How does God intend for you to find your true value?

2. If it's true that your husband doesn't control your feelings, why does his behavior elicit those feelings in you? What is the true source of those feelings?

3. How do you see yourself at this moment? Where did you derive your conclusions about who you are and what you are like?

4. How does God describe you? Do your feelings about your value come mostly from God or your husband? How close or far apart are the ways each of them sees you?

5. How does a wife command respect?

Chapter 5: Bible Bangers

1. A comedian mentioned in this chapter used the word "oversaved" to describe someone who acts hyper-religious. How might an "oversaved" wife act, and how might those actions be harmful?

2. A man doesn't have to look religious to be a godly husband. Do you agree or disagree? Why?

3. What is legalism, and how do wives sometimes try to impose legalism on their husbands? Why is this harmful rather than helpful?

4. God isn't waiting for your husband to change in order to accept and love him. How might you express your acceptance of your husband at this very moment, right where he is in his own spiritual walk?

Chapter 6: Soured Saints

1. Have you and your husband faced a catastrophic loss together? Describe how you saw or didn't see God in the midst of that situation. Has your view of the circumstance changed over time? If you haven't faced a situation like this, have you known another couple who did? How did they handle it?

2. If a husband is antagonistic toward faith in Christ, his wife may sometimes feel as if she is a failure. What might cause these feelings? What advice would you give to this wife?

3. Peter once stood between Jesus and the cross, which was the Father's will for Him. In what ways might a wife stand in the way of what God is doing in her husband's life?

4. How is a wife to react when her husband says negative things about God? Why should we resist the temptation to defend God?

5. When a husband vents his pain by saying untrue things about God, should a wife validate his feelings? Why or why not?

Chapter 7: Unholy Ghosts

1. What is authentic grace?

2. How does grace come into focus when the opportunity to do wrong arises?

3. How is a wife to respond when her husband encourages her to follow him in sinful choices? What is she to do if he insists?

4. What helpful response could a wife give her husband when he insists that she do something sinful?

Chapter 8: Confronting Bullies

1. What are some of the ways that husbands bully their wives? What is a healthy attitude for a Christian wife to have about being bullied?

2. How does grace cause an abused woman to respond toward her husband's bad behavior? Describe some specific responses that would be appropriate.

3. How do wives often react inappropriately when their husbands bully them?

4. What is the key to gaining your husband's respect?

Chapter 9: Trash Talk

1. What might happen when a wife oversteps proper boundaries in the way she talks about her husband to her friends?

2. What is the first thing that a woman should do if she begins to feel resentment?

3. If you are being asked for advice or comfort, how should you respond?

4. How do your words affect your attitude and actions toward your husband?

5. Describe a healthy way to approach your husband with grievances.

6. What is the goal in dialogue when there are problems in your relationship to your husband?

Chapter 10: Greener Grass

1. What are the three most basic needs of every human being? Define those needs in your own words.

2. What is emotional adultery? Is this as serious as physical adultery? Can one exist apart from the other?

3. What are some of the warning signs that an inappropriate

relationship is developing? How can you avoid this kind of extramarital relationship?

4. Is there any truth to the statement, "I didn't mean for it to happen"? What is the correct response to this statement?

Chapter 11: Rearing Children

1. What is the effect on the home when a husband and wife do not have a unified approach to child rearing?

2. What are some ways you and your husband can show your children a united front? How might a child try to play one against the other? How should you respond?

3. What are the differences between teaching children how to behave and teaching them about their identity? Why is teaching children their identity the more important of the two?

4. You can give your children more than a good image. In what ways can teaching them to have a biblical image prepare them for the future?

Chapter 12: Festering Wounds

1. What effect does time have on deep emotional wounds? Does time heal all wounds?

2. List some common misunderstandings about forgiveness.

3. What is an accurate definition of forgiveness?

4. Isaiah 43:25 says that God forgives us for His own sake. Why is it important to forgive others for your own sake? How does forgiving those who have hurt you help you?

5. What does the Bible mean when it says God will not remember your sins? What is the difference between that and forgetting your sins?

6. How can a person move past the pain of adultery?

7. Forgiveness isn't fair to the one who was hurt, but it is an integral part of grace. Do you agree or disagree? Why?

Chapter 13: Religious Arguments

1. What is the best thing to do when being provoked into an argument?

2. What is the difference between arguing and debating?

3. What is the difference between reacting to people and responding to them? Why is it important to respond and not react?

4. If somebody speaks negatively about God, why is it not necessary to defend Him? What is a better response to the person who criticizes?

5. How can we validate people's painful feelings without affirming their untrue words?

Chapter 14: Other Voices

1. Knowing that your marriage is a gift from God, how would you choose a confidant?

2. How can you know you are receiving godly advice?

3. Before you begin talking to others about your husband, listen to your heavenly Father. What kind of things are you likely to hear Him say to you?

4. Having a God-given confidant is important, but what should you beware of when you talk about your husband?

Chapter 15: Clean Fights

1. What is the difference between constructive and destructive words when you argue with your husband? Why are words that belittle so dangerous? What is the difference between addressing behavior and attacking character?

2. What is wrong with the idea that one person knows the other said certain things only because the other person was angry and didn't really mean it?

3. How should a wife respond if her husband puts her down in a way that attempts to diminish her as a person?

4. What are a few helpful guidelines for disagreements in marriage?

5. Why is it more important to reach understanding than agreement when you differ with your mate? What are some helpful ways to facilitate understanding?

Chapter 16: Juggling Acts

1. In what ways does contemporary society communicate to wives that they should be able to handle all the responsibilities thrust upon them? What effect does this unrealistic message have on women?

2. What woman do you know who seems to juggle all the responsibilities in her life perfectly? How does this comparison cause you to feel? If you were to ask her how she perfectly manages it all, what do you imagine she would say? Do you really believe her lifestyle fits the perception you have of her?

3. In what ways can you seek your family's help with household responsibilities? How can your husband and children help? When do you plan to talk to them about this need, and what do you plan to say? (It is important to think this through before you take this step.)

4. Do wives have more duties today than they did a generation ago? Two generations? In what ways? How have wives adapted to these changes?

5. Describe the difference between excellence and perfection. How will you reach for excellence without falling into the trap of believing you must achieve perfection?

6. What are some things you can eliminate from your busy life? How will you respond to those who are unhappy with your decision to press the delete button on some things in order to make your lifestyle more manageable?

Chapter 17: Prodigal Sons

1. Have you ever discovered that your child made a decision that

violated all you have taught him at home? How did you handle it? If your children are still young, how do you imagine you would handle it?

2. What is the harm in obsessing with the question of "why?" when our children make bad decisions? In what ways is the question counterproductive?

3. What is your role regarding your child's behavior?

4. What does it mean to find your "emotional equilibrium" when your child has made bad choices?

5. Discuss this statement in light of a wrong choice your child has made: God's grace is bigger than our wrong choices.

Chapter 18: Blended Families

1. In what ways can parents who are planning their second marriage help prepare their children for being in a blended family?

2. What can one do to help facilitate the growth of love in the relationship with a stepchild?

3. Discuss the best way to handle the discipline of the children in a blended family.

4. What are some lessons that children can learn about God from being in a blended family?

Chapter 19: Unscrambling Eggs

1. Describe how God's grace shows itself to be bigger than the foolish and immature choices we may make in life. Use an example from your own life.

2. What does it mean to forgive yourself for your own past failures? Why is it important to forgive yourself?

3. Formulate a statement that affirms that your heavenly Father loves your child and that His love will shape your child more than your past failures will. Write it down and then read it aloud.

Chapter 20: Physical Abuse

1. What are some of the early signs in a dating relationship that a man is likely to be physically abusive later? How should these indicators be handled?

2. How does a wife hurt her husband by tolerating physical abuse from him? Explain why God does not want her to be passive and allow such a thing to happen.

3. What kind of internal change must a wife experience in order to realize that she does not deserve to be abused? How does she need to come to see God? Herself? Her husband's behavior?

4. What actions can a wife take to become proactive about stopping the abuse? How does faith in Christ and His grace operating in her help her to be bold and proactive? Why is it a sin for her to continue to allow such behavior?

5. Where can an abused wife find support and practical assistance? What should she say to her husband about the physical abuse? When should she leave him?

Chapter 21: Emotional Absence

1. What are some reasons why a husband might be emotionally absent from his wife?

2. What are three common ways wives try to get their unresponsive husbands to communicate? Why don't these attempts work?

3. Describe how to talk to your husband about your feelings in a way that ensures you are heard. What helpful communication techniques are discussed in this chapter?

4. What biblical truths can encourage you in knowing that your husband's aloof stance isn't because something is wrong with you? How can you find encouragement in your relationship to your Father in heaven?

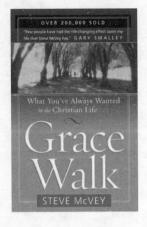
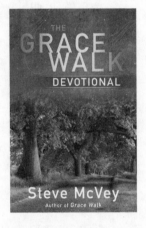

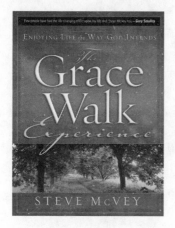

The Grace Walk Experience

Steve McVey's popular *Grace Walk* has inspired thousands of Christians to leave behind a performance-based faith and to embrace God's abundant purpose and life. *The Grace Walk Experience* workbook helps you apply eight truths that have changed lives worldwide, understand your identity in Christ, and rest in God's grace.

Helping Others Overcome Addictions
Steve McVey and Mike Quarles

These addiction-breaking biblical truths will make all the difference for you or someone you love. Freedom from addiction comes only when you fully believe what God says about your identity, get radically right with Him, and dwell in your identity in Christ. This helpful manual includes material on codependency and recovery-support groups.

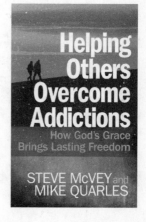

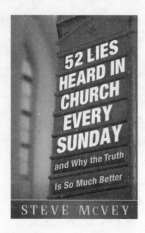

52 Lies Heard in Church Every Sunday

Steve shows how pastors and churches can distort scriptural truths because of preconceptions and end up diminishing the loving, *personal* God, who gives you everything in Christ. The problems Steve examines include ignoring part of the truth and confusing our role with God's. He guides you to a closer, more fulfilling relationship with Him.

Walking in the Will of God

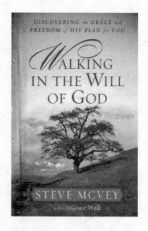

Steve helps frustrated Christians rediscover the grace-filled, relational God of the Scriptures and demonstrates that a rule-focused life causes anxiety and distance from the Father. Conversely, a relationship-based life brings security in His dependability. When you know God *wants* to guide you, you can relax and enjoy a bold, no-regrets life.